SIX CRIMINAL WOMEN

SIX CRIMINAL WOMEN

by

ELIZABETH JENKINS

Biography Index Reprint Series

BOOKS FOR LIBRARIES PRESS
FREEPORT, NEW YORK

Copyright © 1949 by Elizabeth Jenkins

Reprinted 1971 by arrangement with
Hawthorn Books, Inc.

INTERNATIONAL STANDARD BOOK NUMBER:
0-8369-8069-7

LIBRARY OF CONGRESS CATALOG CARD NUMBER:
76-148222

PRINTED IN THE UNITED STATES OF AMERICA

FOREWORD

I must acknowledge a debt of gratitude to *Twelve Bad Women,* Fisher Unwin, 1897, edited by Arthur Vincent. It was the essays in this book on Alice Perrers by Mr. Arthur Vincent and Jane Webb by Mr. Charles Andrews that showed me for the first time how interesting these two subjects were and made me want to read about them for myself.

I should also like to say how much I relied, in writing about Lady Essex, on the exhaustive bibliography supplied by Sir Philip Gibbs in his life of Robert Carr, *King's Favourite,* Hutchinson, 1909.

I was attracted to the Lady Theodosia Ivie by Sir John C. Fox's edition of *The Lady Ivie's Trial for great part of Shadwell in the county of Middlesex.* Clarendon Press, 1929.

I do not remember where I first heard of Madame Rachel Leverson, but I am indebted to Mr. William Roughead's version in *Bad Companions* for knowledge of the pamphlet: *The Extraordinary Life and Trial of Madame Sarah Rachel Leverson,* of which, by great good luck, I managed to secure a copy.

No one could undertake to write anything about the Balham Mystery without the aid of Sir John Hall's book: *The Bravo Mystery and other Cases,* Bodley Head, 1923. The other source for this story is the exceptionally interesting pamphlet: *The Balham Mystery,* British Museum Reading Room, 1891, d33.

With the exception of the Lady Ivie, who, so far as I know, has never been treated of at length, although Dr. M. R. James wrote one of his ghost stories about her

Foreword

(*A Neighbour's Landmark*), some, at least, of these remaining five stories will be familiar to the reader; but I believe that those who know a good story best are usually the ones most ready to hear it again, and, secondly, that as ideas and tastes are always changing, however often a contemporary source of material has been used, those who go back to it can almost always find something, previously ignored or discarded, to offer their own generation.

CONTENTS

	PAGE
Foreword	v
Madame Sarah Rachel Leverson	1
Alice Perrers	31
The Lady Ivie	57
Frances Howard, Countess of Somerset	81
Jane Webb	137
The Balham Mystery	177

MADAME SARAH RACHEL LEVERSON

The practice of make-up is infinitely old, and some even of its methods remain unchanged. What alters is the attitude of the public towards it. Our own day is probably the first in all history to accept it as a commonplace for almost every type of female, of every age and in every station of life.

In every age but our own the written utterance of men has been against it. Shakespeare makes Hamlet say: "God gave you one face and you make yourselves another." Ben Jonson, following the Roman satirists, complained of women who plaster themselves at night with oil and bird-lime and "lie in of a new face". The poet Crashawe seems to have suffered from lip-rouge. In "The not-impossible She" he hoped to find

Lips where all day
A lover's kiss may play
And nothing take away.

Congreve makes Mr. Mirabell lay down in the marriage conditions he makes with Millamant: "That you continue to like your own face as long as I shall, and while 'it passes current with me, you endeavour not to new' coin it." The Vicar of Wakefield contrived to upset into the fire a pan in which his daughters were making a face-wash. In short, masculine disapproval of cosmetics appears to have been general and consistent. But with the Victorian age the disapproval took on a new quality. In other ages men had complained of cosmetics because they made women unsavoury, or because they denoted worldliness or immorality, or because their use made old women ridiculous, but the subtle charge of impropriety was a development of the nineteenth century. Even the fierce denunciations of the mediaeval Church, with their talk of whores and hell-fire, had never achieved the gravity of Victorian censure. The Victorians' attitude to sexual immorality was all their own. Previous eras had spoken the most outright condemnation of fornication and adultery, but the Victorian condemnation added an indescribable tone of shamefulness and grief. The impulse of frank abuse of the eighteenth century, for instance, was replaced, in the nineteenth century, by a convention that sexual immorality simply could not be mentioned in ordinary society. Similarly, the practice of painting the face, which was associated with laying out to attract men, was regarded during several decades of the nineteenth century with an almost religious horror. The ideas of maquillage and vice were inseparable. As early as 1833 the unhappy Mrs. Norton complained that a witness for the prosecution in the trial of Norton *v.* Melbourne falsely accused her of "painting and sinning".

Nevertheless, human nature being the same in this era as in any other, painting the face was carried on to some extent. The first flight of fashionable society has always made its own rules and refused to be bound by those of the masses. Here a certain amount of discreet make-up was practised. In *The Eustace Diamonds*, of 1876, Trollope describes the young and lovely but somewhat battered little Lady Eustace as taking to paint. "Through the paleness there was the faintest possible tinge of pink colour shining through the translucent pearl powder. Anyone who knew Lizzie would be sure that when she did paint, she would paint well."

The evidence of a best-selling novelist is always significant, and "Ouida" in *Moths*, 1880, and *The Massarenes*, 1890, makes it clear that fashionable beauties, except the high-minded ones, relied a great deal on Piver. Even so, maquil-

Madame Sarah Rachel Leverson

lage had not become the uniform which every type now adopts, just as everyone wears shoes and stockings. Ouida's day regarded paint as an inferior substitute for natural loveliness. She says of Mouse Kenilworth, who finds, in the height of her beauty, that her harassing intrigue with the odious Massarene is beginning to tell on her: "Each day she was obliged to have a little more recourse to the aids of art. She knew well enough that, however brilliant may be artificial loveliness, it is never quite the same as the radiance of that natural beauty which can affront the drenching rain of a hunting field or the scorching sun on a yacht deck, or, most difficult to bear of all, the clear light of early day after a ball." Today, needless to say, the beautiful woman outshines the plain one as she has always done; but she paints as automatically as the other. She does not paint because her looks are going; she paints in "the morn and liquid dew of youth". Indeed, the "stock-broker's dream" complexion is only achieved by putting a layer of paint on a skin in its first youthful perfection.

The alteration in the general attitude to make-up is undoubtedly caused by men. Men may say, and perhaps mean, that they dislike the sight of gouts of crimson lard left on tea-cups, on cigarette-ends, on handkerchiefs and fingertips and on their own shirt collars, but masculine approval of paint is not only obvious from the women with whom men like to be seen, but it might be taken for granted. In a society where women seriously outnumber men, the great majority of the sex would not adopt a practice that men found unpleasant. This change in men's attitude is probably one of the results of the emancipation of women. Most men, however much they may approve of it intellectually, are emotionally chilled by feminism, and a lavish use of paint seems to them a welcome gesture in the opposite direction. Now that it has become adopted as a uniform, numberless women naturally use it without any consciousness of its implication, but in itself paint does suggest a readiness to admit sexual advances. Our age is perhaps the first since the fall of the Roman Empire in which a man can find sexual indulgence in any walk of female society.

In the nineteenth century the opposite condition ruled. Though instances of immorality were found among the ranks of respectable women, they were markedly exceptional, and when discovered they were punished by social ostracism. At this time, the great majority of women were entirely unassisted in their looks. The woman whose skin did not become greasy, whose nose did not turn red, whose lips and cheeks had a good natural colour, appeared radiant indeed among less fortunate contemporaries. One can appreciate the meaning of the phrase so often found in nineteenth-century novels, when the heroine, dressing for an occasion, is "in remarkably good looks": a blessing indeed to a girl who could not conceal a red nose under a foundation lotion or mask a shiny one with powder.

An exceedingly popular novelist whose long career was contemporary with Ouida's gives what seems the oddest reason ever advanced against artificial aids to beauty. Charlotte Yonge, in *Womankind,* says that their use by plain women is an injustice to the beautiful. Miss Yonge, though a writer with a very large public, was unusually high-minded, and many even of her contemporary readers must have disagreed with her here. But the fact of her making such a remark implies that it was representative to a certain degree. It is inconceivable that in our own day it could be made at all.

The manufacture of cosmetics must have improved rapidly in the last three decades of the nineteenth century, if Ouida's tributes to Piver were deserved, for up till the 1850s at least the choice was small and the colours crude. There were rouges and red salve for the lips, black kohl for the eyes. Women of the eighteenth century had covered their face and

Madame Sarah Rachel Leverson

neck with a substance called ceruse. It was made of white lead, and women had been known to die from assimilating the poison through the pores of the skin. In the nineteenth century ceruse had been superseded by pearl powder, which, though less startling as it was transparent, was still of unnatural pallor. The infinite variety of tints in rouge and powder, cream and eye-shadow offered today, including the claim of certain advertisers to blend a powder for the colour of each individual face, was entirely unknown. While any trace of natural freshness remained, women were probably better off without the clown's make-up of red, white and black.

But the anxiety to be well married, or at least safely married, the rivalry of other women, the pangs of despised love, of jealousy, the chill terror of advancing time, all these woes and pains were as poignant as they are with us, and scarcely anyone had exploited them! What a harvest was waiting for the genius who could see it!

In 1863 there opened at 47a New Bond Street a small shop, over which, with surprisingly modern technique, was written in gold lettering, "Beautiful for Ever". The shop, small, elegant and bright, stationed in the stream of one of the most fashionable streets in London, had an almost magical shimmer in the eyes of the passers-by. It had not only the atmosphere of luxurious expensiveness for which Bond Street is still famous, but it promised in its depths something occult and infinitely desired; it held a mysterious gem-like radiance like Aladdin's cave. Two young ladies, Miss Rachel and Miss Leonte Leverson, attended the clients in the front part of the shop. Behind, in a small parlour, the proprietress presided: Mrs. Sarah Rachel Leverson, known to fame as Madame Rachel.

This extraordinary being had not, at first glance, the appearance one would expect of a beauty specialist. She was tall, corpulent and bold-featured, and, though richly dressed, had no pretentions to beauty of her own. She was in fact both formidable and repellent, but the effect she created in the weaker minds of her clients was the more powerful. They received the impression that here was a woman of supernormal abilities. The toy of beauty, which they themselves desired, was of no personal interest to her, but she could sell it to them as she would sell a phial of Arabian perfume or a box of violet cachous.

Madame Rachel had two ostensible lines of business. One dealt in articles of make-up. She supplied face creams with evocative names, such as Arabian Cream and Senses of Peace; Indian and Egyptian kohl for darkening the eyebrows, lashes and lids; red paste for the lips; and various kinds of rouges; Circassian Golden Hair Wash; fragrant mouth washes; dentifrice; and Royal Bridal Bath Soap at two guineas a tablet. Her "washes for the complexion", of which she advertised ten, included Pure Extracts of the China Rose, Alabaster Liquid, and Armenian Liquid for Removing Wrinkles. For the mouth she sold Tooth Enamel, Arabian Perfume Wash, Pearly Tooth Powder and Balmy Reed Powder. Her Youth and Beauty Cream and Roseate Unguent afford two more examples of her happy skill in names, to which might be added Peach Blossom Soap and Alabaster Soap, each of which cost two guineas a tablet. She showed her appreciation of the bogus scientific approach, of which her descendants have made good use, by such titles as: Preservative Cream, Medicated Cream for rendering the hair black or chestnut brown, Astringents and Stimulants for rendering the hair Italian brown, and Arabian Fumigated Oils. Above all, she sold tinted face powder. It is an open question whether the tint "Rachel" is so called after Madame Rachel or after the tragedienne Rachel Felix, of whom Madame kept a bust on her premises and to whom she said she was related. At all events, Madame, if she did not invent it, was one of the earliest to sell it, and its influence on the clients must have been very remarkable. The woman who,

Madame Sarah Rachel Leverson

having known nothing but chalk white powder, saw herself for the first time made up with Rachel powder, would think the improvement so extraordinary she might well credit the vendeuse with unique abilities.

The second line of business was of the remedial kind. None of Madame's preparations, of which there were upwards of sixty, cost less than a guinea, but the prices of the "cures" were breathtaking. This was not surprising, seeing that they claimed to impart the gift that women have been longing after since the beginning of the world. The virtues of these special preparations were set forth in a pamphlet, published in 1863. This work was enticing even to look at. It was bound in a stiff cover of glossy rose-pink, and bore the title *Beautiful for Ever!* It was indeed a very remarkable production and one of the earliest masterpieces of modern advertising. Madame Rachel wished among other things to recommend a practice that was considered thoroughly dubious to the more or less respectable women of the moneyed class. The tone of the pamphlet is rhapsodizing and high-faluting, and recommends beauty culture almost in the light of a sacred duty.

"Our first mother of the world, who claimed our love and pity for her beauty and her sorrow, was a beautiful woman. From the beginning of the world, she was the companion of man in youth and his solace in age. She is man's guiding star, gentle, loving woman, who by her gentle counsel leads men on to deeds of greatness and renown." The pamphlet goes on to celebrate the charm and purity of Queen Victoria, with a retrospective glance at the Duchess of Kent, passing references to the Princess Royal, Princess Alice and Princess Alexandra of Denmark, and pays tribute to the mental qualities of Grace Darling and Florence Nightingale. But after commemorating so much respectability and moral worth, the pamphlet glides, as it were, imperceptibly into its true vein.

Six Criminal Women

"However the charms of mind may be extolled, it is most essential to ladies that personal attractions should be blended with them." The weapon of which the modern advertiser makes so much use, that of terrifying the potential customer with the threat of perpetual spinsterhood because of halitosis, perspiration odour or sagging busts, was already used by Madame though couched in the idiom of a politer age. It was regrettable, said the pamphlet, that the world was very unkind in its comments on plain and unattractive women, but it was also undeniably true, and many women who were conscious of deficient or failing charms were so much afraid of sneering comments that they lacked confidence to make the promenade of the ballroom on a partner's arm. "It is our endeavour to prove that a lady cannot be too careful in the arrangement of her toilet, as the future happiness of her life may depend upon her first appearance in society."

No reader was likely to deny this; the point was, what should be done about it? Madame supplied the answer in words which again foreshadowed the modern technique in their blend of sound psychology and scientific humbug. After saying that the first step in all beauty treatment is to make sure there is no stomachic derangement, she goes on to describe and advocate her chef d'œuvre, the Arabian bath.

This must not be confused with the Turkish bath, which in its sudden transitions from hot to cold is far too violent for the fragile female constitution. "In fact, instances have been known," asserts the pamphlet, "in which the Turkish baths have proved too powerful for the constitution of horses." No! The Arabian bath was a different creation altogether. Madame Rachel's method of beautifying did not consist "in stopping up the pores of the flesh with dangerous cosmetics, neither was it in plastering up the skin by painting the face. . . . On the contrary, it was accomplished by the use of the Arabian bath, composed

Madame Sarah Rachel Leverson

of pure extracts of the liquid of flowers, choice and rare herbs and other ingredients equally harmless and efficacious".

The use of the bath was supplemented by applications of Magnetic Rock Dew Water of the Sahara. The pamphlet recalled (what was the fact) that seventeen years before, in 1846, the *Illustrated London News* had published an article on the toilet preparations used in the East and had described the Magnetic Dew in these words: "In the interior of the Sahara is a magnetic rock from which water distils sparingly in the form of dew, which is possessed of extraordinary property. Whether a latent electricity be imparted by magnetism, or an additional quantity of oxygen enters into its composition, it is not easy to say." This water, it was now revealed, was sold by Madame at 47a New Bond Street, she having acquired the sole right of importation "at enormous outlay" from the Moroccan government. The water would "increase the vital energies, restore the colour of grey hair, give the appearance of youth to persons far advanced in years and remove wrinkles, defects and blemishes".

Another of the washes was called Jordan Water, and another Toilet of Venus.

Although Madame said on one page that in her treatment she did not stop up the pores and plaster the face, on a subsequent page she revealed that this was exactly what she did, for she announced herself as an enameller. Any possible objections to this practice were firmly put down: "In endeavouring to remove the delusion that the process is accomplished by injurious cosmetics and other compounds destructive to health and beauty, we beg to assure our fair readers that the process of enamelling is conducive to health and beauty, grace and youth." Her treatment not only conferred beauty, but was "conducive to health. . . . Health is as great an auxiliary to beauty as is a pure mind to an innocent face".

Six Criminal Women

The prices of these treatments were naturally very high. The Magnetic Rock Dew Water cost ten guineas a flask and Jordan Water was from five to ten guineas. A course of baths cost from fifty to five hundred guineas. A complete beauty treatment including the full range of cosmetics was called The Royal Bridal Toilet Cabinet as arranged by Madame Rachel for the Sultaness of Turkey and copied by her for the Royal Brides of Europe. This cost one thousand guineas.

There was, indeed, plenty of money "about". The aristocracy had not yet outlived its wealth, and the moneyed classes had received immense augmentation from the ranks of the merchants. Opulence was reflected in the elaboration and richness of ornament and design. Dress, in the 1860s, while it retained the last lingering wraith of gracefulness which was to disappear for good with the coming of the '70s was becoming heavier and richer, to the detriment of its beauty. The wide hooped skirt and small tight bodice of the preceding decades were there still, in outline, but the hoop was developing a jutting rear like a bird's tail, and the small jackets were breaking out into braid, tassels, frogs and bows. There was, however, a certain graceful audacity, which had not yet become vulgar showiness. Skirts were sometimes looped up to show the ankles; hats were charming, either flat round straws like a target, or small pill-boxes with a quill. Bonnets were still small and sat on the back of the head and were tied with a large bow under the chin. As they gave the countenance no shade, they had often a lace veil, spangled. The throng that streamed through Bond Street bore the stamp of a sophisticated, daring, and, above all, moneyed age. The exploiter cannot arise until the time is ripe.

The birth date of Sara Rachel Leverson is given variously as 1806 and 1823. At all events, in 1863 she was well on in life. Of her first husband one thing only is known, but

Madame Sarah Rachel Leverson

that one is significant. He was a chemist's assistant. From him, no doubt, Madame gained her insight into compounding and bottling. On his death, she moved from Manchester to London. Here she sold old clothes, and at one time kept a fried-fish-shop in Clare Market. Another activity which must have developed her power of ascendancy over other minds was telling fortunes. This she did for a penny a time.

She married again, a Mr. Moses, but he was drowned at sea in 1859. Finally she married a Mr. Philip Leverson, and settled with him in some comfort at 25 Dean Street. Before her story became public, Mr. Leverson also had disappeared. This was not surprising. Madame was of the type which outlasts many husbands.

By one or other of her previous marriages she had seven children. Two remained with her. Their names were Rachel and Leonte. The former, a handsome and collected young creature, clearly inherited some of her mama's ability. It was she who composed the brochure *Beautiful for Ever*. If she also invented the slogan, hers was one of the earliest master-minds in advertising.

At some period before 1860 Madame was taken with what the Victorians called "the fever", whether scarlet, cholera or typhoid, and was removed to King's College Hospital, where they shaved her head. The loss of her abundant black hair, her only beauty, caused her passionate distress. To soothe her, the house surgeon promised her a lotion which would make it grow again as well as ever. The lotion was produced and applied and her hair did indeed grow again. It grew like Samson's, and Madame, all gratitude, begged the doctor to give her the prescription. This he did. It may have contained some simple ingredients, or it may have been coloured water. Nothing was needed to promote a vigorous growth of hair on such a head. Madame Rachel was so illiterate that she could not write even her own name, but her intelligence was exceptional. She had the prescription in her hand and a new growth of hair on her head. It did not take her long to understand that the two were quite unconnected; but she remembered, no doubt, her own agitation and dismay as she lay in the hospital bed, and how miraculously she had been soothed by the application of the lotion and the assurance that it would have the desired effect. It is not too much to say that in the good-natured doctor's prescription she had the key to the whole vast edifice of the modern beauty racket. The key had been lying in other people's sight for long enough. She was the first to recognize it and to make a fortune by it.

Her first attempts were not successful. She set up as an enameller in Paris and then in Brighton, and then in New Bond Street. The pink pamphlet refers guardedly to there having been a lawsuit, presumably begun by Madame, in connection with a client who would not pay, in which judgment was given for the latter. The pamphlet points out that it was never in dispute that the beautifying process had been successful. The client had bilked an honest and industrious practitioner on some legal flaw in the contract. Obviously there had been troubles. The first venture in New Bond Street ended in bankruptcy and Madame served a short term in Whitecross Prison. But her confidence in the future of the line she had chosen was undaunted by a few false starts. The alluring pamphlet in its shiny, sugar-pink cover sold at half a crown, was widely disseminated to advertise the new beginning. In 47a New Bond Street, under its gilt legend, success kindled at last.

The outstanding difference between the case of Madame Rachel and her hair tonic, and that of a dissatisfied client of Madame's own, and one of Madame's preparations, was of course the difference between success and failure. The confidence in the illusion was the same, but in one instance nature could achieve her result on a healthy, vital organism, in another the subject would be too old or too much de-

Madame Sarah Rachel Leverson

vitalized for nature to succeed. These cases were bound to occur, and, in a clientele as large as Madame's, to occur pretty frequently. Her promises were so large and her prices so high, that, where her failure was obvious, the client threatened to become quite unmanageable. How then did Madame manage to cover up these failures from the eyes of the world and maintain the stream of fees into her bank account? For no reverses seemed to check her. There are people alive today whose parents saw her driving in Hyde Park behind a pair of high-stepping bays. In 1867 she took a box at Covent Garden for the season for four hundred pounds. Her house was in Maddox Street, an address that spoke for itself, and Miss Rachel and Miss Leonte, though they worked in the shop, had dresses, jewels, singing lessons and advantages in general as if they were born inhabitants of Belgravia.

The secret of Madame's success with a client who threatened to expose her was a simple one. When some infuriated great lady threatened an action against her, Madame dropped the mask of scientific beauty specialist. Her servile graciousness disappeared also. Only the power was left, and that took on a new form. With an odious, leering familiarity, a hideously derisive laugh, she would remind the customer that if the matter appeared in court everyone would know that the lady had been taking beauty treatments! "The ugliest old woman in London that even Madame Rachel can do nothing for!" cried Madame in horrid glee.

Though none of us would enjoy an encounter with Madame Rachel, it would be quite impossible for her to blackmail us by such a threat. No one today feels compromised or made ridiculous by a visit to one of the discreet salons which have replaced Madame's original venture. But that the threat was actually effective in the 1860s we can tell from various pieces of evidence of the time. One of these is the remarkable passage in *David Copperfield* (1852), in which little Miss Mowcher explains that great ladies won't admit that they use rouge even to the person from whom they buy it: "One Dowager . . . she calls it gloves. Another, *she* calls it tucker edging. Another, *she* calls it a fan. *I* call it whatever *they* call it. I supply it for 'em, but we keep up the trick so to one another, and make believe with such a face, that they'd as soon think of laying it on before a whole drawing-room as before me."

Besides the threat of being made to look ridiculous, worldly and improper, Madame's hostility carried with it a menace of something absolutely disreputable, such as might deter clients even today. Significant though implicit evidence of this is found in the anecdote of Admiral C., quoted in Sergeant Ballantyne's *Memoirs*. The Admiral's wife made some purchases at 47a New Bond Street and paid for them. Some time afterwards, she received a bill for one thousand pounds. In astonishment she asked Madame what it could be for. Madame first brazenly told her it was for beauty treatments and when Mrs. C. denied having had anything for which she had not paid already, Madame threatened to tell the lady's husband "everything". Unfortunately, Madame had for once mistaken her quarry. Mrs. C. immediately told her husband the whole affair and Admirel C. effectively put a stop to Madame's attempts at extortion.

Much less happy was the episode of a nameless lady, related by Mr. Montagu Williams, Q.C. (*Leaves of a Life*). This client, when she undressed to take an Arabian bath, put her diamond rings and ear-rings into a dressing-table drawer. When she went to put them on again they were not there. The lady rushed into the parlour behind the shop where Madame sat and angrily demanded her diamonds. With instant, brutal effrontery Madame exclaimed:

"It's no use your giving yourself airs here! I know who you are—I have had you watched. How would you like

Madame Sarah Rachel Leverson

your husband to know the real reason of your coming here, and about the gentleman who has visited you here?" The agitated, terrified woman lost her head completely. She hurried from the shop and never reappeared, leaving her diamonds in Madame's hands.

The angry and cheated women were those who bought the expensive cures. Madame made her large sums out of these wares; it was stated afterwards that in a good year she made as much as twenty thousand pounds; but her fame and her hold on the public confidence rested on the fact that she sold good paint, and made a certain number of her clients look much better than they did before. Judging again by that sensitive barometer, the popular novel, she had become really famous as a beauty specialist. In *Lady Audley's Secret* (1864), the authoress exclaims: "Imagine all the women of England elevated to the high level of masculine intellectuality, superior to pearl powder and Mrs. Rachel Leverson"; and again, of the confidential lady's maid: "She knows when the sweet smile is more false than Madame Leverson's enamel, and far less enduring—when the words that issue from between gates of borrowed pearl are more disguised and painted than the lips which helped to shape them." While some years later her slogan had for the time being at least become part of the language. In *The Eustace Diamonds* Trollope describes the complexion of Mrs. Carbuncle as of so vivid a red and white that people who did not know her declared that she must have been made "beautiful for ever".

Had Madame Rachel been content to let well alone, to be satisfied with her enormous gains, she might have gone on amassing one fortune after another, using her cunning and her strength of mind to overcome such minor mishaps as were inevitable, and keeping unimpaired a steady flow of income from the majority of her clients. Unfortunately, like many criminals, she had not the artist's gift of knowing when to stop. Bloated with the exercise of power, and made reckless by success, she started on the downward path which, with one temporary halt, led her to the pit of absolute ruin.

There came to her in 1867 a client who was so complete an example of the female situation which she lived to exploit that Madame must have felt like an expert cracksman confronted with a child's money-box. Mrs. Borrodaile was the widow of a distinguished Indian Army officer. She was never prevailed on to give her age, but, as she admitted that she had been married in 1846, she was probably between forty-five and fifty. She was that deplorable object, the once pretty idiot who is no longer pretty. She had been captivating, and had enjoyed a radiant youth. When her looks faded, she had nothing to live for. Querulous and absurd, she was a burden to herself and an exasperation to her family. She had chosen to separate herself from all her relatives, including her daughter. They were uncongenial to her. They did not realize, probably, that if one is a beauty one has a right to special consideration and is not quite on the same plane as other people.

Mrs. Borrodaile was able to be independent. She had a little property at Streatham, five thousand pounds' worth of stock, and an army pension of three hundred pounds a year. This was enough to put her in peril from the sharks, and her position was made acutely dangerous by her being out of touch with her relations.

Mrs. Borrodaile appears to have been as nearly devoid of intelligence as it is possible to be without getting oneself shut up. But it must be borne in mind that though the standard of general intelligence probably remains the same from age to age, the standard of general information, in the female sex particularly, has improved considerably in the last hundred years. A woman of Mrs. Borrodaile's mentality, living today, would, despite herself, have acquired a certain degree of worldly wisdom. Even so, the newspapers bring

Madame Sarah Rachel Leverson

up from time to time instances of ignorance and gullibility which quite stagger us. Some of these must be remembered when we find it almost impossible to credit Mrs. Borrodaile's story.

Mrs. Borrodaile entered Madame Rachel's web and instantly fell a prey to the powerful mind in the centre of it. Madame said it was clear that Mrs. Borrodaile had had unusual beauty and there would be no difficulty in restoring it. She provided the client with expensive soaps and lotions and prescribed a course of the famous Arabian baths. These skilful and costly treatments were not administered on the premises. They were to be had "round the corner" in Davies Street, at the house of a Mrs. Hickes. Here a dressing-room was provided for the clients, and the baths were taken in a tin tub in a wooden shed. Madame had warned Mrs. Borrodaile that improvement would not be immediate, but she professed to see signs of it in Mrs. Borrodaile before the usual time. Mrs. Borrodaile, always optimistic about her appearance and perfectly ready to believe in improvement, would have been quite willing to leave the matter in Madame's hands. It was not her confidence that failed, but her banking account. After a course of baths, she told Madame regretfully that for the present she could afford nothing further.

Then Madame sprang the trap.

The one remnant of sense which Mrs. Borrodaile retained from those happy days, when an able man had taken care of her, was that one must never sell one's capital. Madame whole-heartedly agreed with this dictum, but she said there was one exception. Capital should be sold, if by that means you could buy a better investment. *That* was how fortunes were made. Clever business men did it every day. She had, she said, an investment to offer to Mrs. Borrodaile of the most brilliant kind. A part of her capital invested in further beauty treatment would bring in such a return of wealth and happiness as Mrs. Borrodaile could scarcely dream of. In short, the latter had made a most important conquest—of none other than Lord Ranelagh.

This nobleman was a figure who would have looked more at home in the period of the Regency than in mid-Victorian society, but he was ideally suited to Madame's purpose. He was a hard-bitten man of the world, a bon viveur, and, though elderly, he had never married. Madame had exaggerated his income to the unsuspicious Mrs. Borrodaile, but though by no means wealthy, he was a well-known member of fashionable society. No more eloquent tribute to the elegance and vogue of Madame's shop could have been paid than the fact that Lord Ranelagh visited it. Whether he bought some uncompromising trifle, perfume, or a vinaigrette for a female friend, or whether it amused him to see who the clients were, at all events he was not unknown at 47a New Bond Street.

Even Mrs. Borrodaile could at first hardly believe that she had captivated such a man. She had never met him, she said. Then Madame told her that Lord Ranelagh had spied upon her through the boards of the bath house, and become enslaved by the sight of her. It was improper, naturally, said Madame. She herself had of course been unaware that the spyhole existed. But one knew what men were. And why regret the incident, when the outcome had been so fortunate?

The wretched dupe was overcome. She felt that her boats were burned; she also felt no further disposition to doubt Madame's assurances. Her agitation mastered, she listened with trembling delight as Madame dilated upon the future that awaited her. Lord Ranelagh, said Madame, had declared that he must and would make Mrs. Borrodaile his wife. But to confirm the favourable impression, above all, to make it lasting, the rest of the beauty treatment must be carried out without delay. Mrs. Borrodaile needed no

Madame Sarah Rachel Leverson

urging. She undertook to have the full course at a cost of one thousand guineas. It was necessary to sell stock for this amount and Madame introduced her own man of business, a Mr. Haynes, for the transaction. Family lawyers are always stuffy, and it is better to keep them out of such matters.

Now began one of the most extraordinary victimisations of one human being by another ever put on record. It is perhaps second only to the Tichborne case as an exploitation, in defiance of all probability, of the force of wishful thinking. That case stands for all time as an example of the power of the mind to believe what it longs to believe. It would have been said that even if the impostor's likeness to the Tichborne heir had been remarkable, the one person on whom he could never have imposed would have been the drowned man's mother. As it was, Lady Tichborne fully accepted an ex-butcher, illiterate, black-bearded and weighing eighteen stone, as her fair, pale, slight, highly bred son. We often say that truth is stranger than fiction. Every now and again we are forced, baffled and bewildered, to believe it.

Madame assured Mrs. Borrodaile that though Lord Ranelagh was burning with devotion, he was obliged to keep the engagement secret from his family until the marriage should take place. They could not therefore meet at present; the courtship must go on by letter. The first of these letters, though its enthusiasm was no doubt gratifying, surprised Mrs. Borrodaile by the illiteracy of its handwriting. And why, she asked, did Ranelagh sign himself William when his name was, in fact, Thomas? Madame instantly replied that owing to a sprained arm Lord Ranelagh had had to dictate to a servant. He was known to his closest intimates as William, because he was so proud of his descent from William the Conqueror. The letters never came to Mrs. Borrodaile's lodging in George Street; they were always handed to her in Madame's shop, and her own replies were written in Madame's parlour, after the shop was closed.

Madame gave her whisky to drink before she began her writing, and it was suggested afterwards in court that it must have been drugged. These evening sessions became more familiar and rank in character as Madame's ascendancy grew ever firmer. Mrs. Borrodaile quickly succumbed to a state that bordered on hypnosis. One evening she was ushered in when Madame was smoking a cigar. Removing it from her lips, Madame handed it to her half-crazed visitor, remarking that it was as warm as Lord Ranelagh's love.

On one occasion Madame actually manœuvred a contact between the supposed lovers. Mrs. Borrodaile was sitting in the parlour behind the shop with another favoured client, when Madame hurried in to them, explaining that she was about to introduce his lordship but Mrs. Borrodaile must pretend to complete ignorance of him. The disguise must at all events be maintained! A moment later she returned with the soldierly, distinguished but somewhat rakish figure. The introduction was made, his lordship spoke a few commonplace remarks and withdrew. His concealment of his feelings had certainly been perfect. On another occasion it was evening and Mrs. Borrodaile was in the parlour. Madame suddenly exclaimed: "Here comes Lord Ranelagh!" and Mrs. Borrodaile saw, in the dim light, a man walk out of the shop. She did not see his face.

Fleeting and inconclusive as these actual meetings might be, the letters made up for them in terms of endearment; they also contained the most emphatic warnings and commands to obey Madame, whom Lord Ranelagh spoke of charmingly as "Granny". Everything, the letters said, depended on Granny's good offices. She not only transmitted their correspondence and forwarded the arrangements for the marriage, but she even rescued his lordship from certain financial entanglements. He ordered Mrs. Borrodaile to repay the old lady. The difficulty was only temporary—he would repay his Mary every shilling; an account should

Madame Sarah Rachel Leverson

be rendered of every farthing. It was clear to Mrs. Borrodaile that her original estimate of Lord Ranelagh's wealth had been a mistaken one, but, to do her justice, this did not diminish her fantastic affection. He was still, with his air, his fashion, his birth, the romantic object of her dreams, and the knowledge of his comparative poverty aroused her tenderness and consideration. Like a daisy root in some vast, low-lit forcing house, towering with luxuriantly tangled creepers, strange, evil orchids and glassy clusters of poisonous fruit, a pure, genuine impulse bloomed in that miasma of hallucination and deceit. She ordered shirts for him, socks and neckties, and offered to see that his linen was washed and mended.

One of the many astonishing facts in the bewitchment of Mrs. Borrodaile was that she was not inexperienced in men's society. She had been married to a distinguished soldier, and in her youth she had been accustomed to the admiration of men. Yet she could accept as the letters of a well-bred man the alarmingly hideous rubbish that Madame's mind naturally produced. "Bear up, my fond one, and I shall be at your feet, those pretty feet that I love, and you may kick your ugly old donkey." Madame invented these grotesque improprieties; but, as she could not write even her own name, they had to be dictated to an amanuensis. When the letters were afterwards produced, they were discovered to be in three different hands. One of these was probably Miss Leonte's, another was that of James Minton, assistant to a linen draper in Holborn, who used to come in and write for Madame after the day's work. The first amanuensis, however, was the one who gave the signature to the whole series. This was an errand boy then in Madame's employ. When he had finished writing out the first letter, the artless lad signed it "William", as that was his own name.

Meantime, under cover of the letters, the skilful robbery of the victim went on fast. Madame's intimacy with Mrs.

Borrodaile and her control of the latter's affairs made it natural that they should buy the trousseau together. It had of course to be of considerable elegance as suited the bride of a peer. Under Madame's guidance Mrs. Borrodaile spent thirty-two pounds on hair ornaments, one hundred and sixty pounds on dresses, another one hundred and sixty pounds on under-linen and four hundred pounds on lace for the wedding dress. All these purchases Madame "took care" of, as she wisely said they were too valuable to leave lying about in George Street. People were so dishonest nowadays you never knew where you were. From Mr. Pike of New Bond Street she helped the bride to choose a diamond coronet and a diamond necklace for one thousand two hundred and sixty pounds. These also Madame took care of. A few days later Madame, unaccompanied this time, took the diamonds back to Mr. Pike and asked for the money back as the lady had changed her mind. The jeweller, deducting one hundred pounds for loss of sale, handed back the balance to Madame Rachel.

At her lodging in George Street, the widow had, as the relics of her past life, a few nice things. She had a set of plate, a silver tea service, some jewellery and some gold seals. Madame, on a visit to George Street, impounded all these. She observed that a peeress would have no use for such commonplace belongings.

Two more frauds of great magnitude and daring she accomplished. She took Mrs. Borrodaile to a carriage builder in New Bond Street and chose a carriage as a present from his bride to the bridegroom. Madame got into the carriage to try it. What a sight her leering features must have presented as she reclined on the rich upholstery! Descending, she said the carriage would do, and gave orders in the bride's name for the Ranelagh arms to be painted on the panels. Then she took her to an empty house in Grosvenor Square. This, she said, was Lord Ranelagh's town house. The bride

Madame Sarah Rachel Leverson

would of course choose the furniture and decorations, and it would be a graceful and appropriate gesture if she paid for them herself. Whether these transactions were turned to Madame's advantage, like that of the diamonds, is not clear. They may have been indulged in simply as a tour de force. It seems likely that she grew to hate her victim because of the latter's utter helplessness.

At all events, the bottom of Mrs. Borrodaile's resources had now been reached. The whole robbery had been accomplished in three months. The speed was of course an essential factor in the success. For this period Mrs. Borrodaile had been buoyed up by a daydream as enthralling as that of an opium addict. Now the charm was rapidly dissolving in the bleak light of inescapable fact. The money was gone, and even Mrs. Borrodaile could not tell herself that she was any the nearer to a marriage with Lord Ranelagh. With her victim's last shilling in her gripe, Madame threw off the last pretence of benevolence. She had, at some point in the pretended negotiations, caused Mrs. Borrodaile to sign a bond undertaking to pay her one thousand, six hundred pounds for the benefit, she said, of Lord Ranelagh. She now demanded the money. The unhappy woman had nothing left with which to pay. Madame had her thrown into gaol for debt. She was taken to Whitecross Prison where Madame herself had once been detained, and only released when she had made over her army pension to Madame Rachel.

In Whitecross Prison she made the acquaintance of a Miss Sutton, and when she was let out this lady accompanied her to 47a New Bond Street. Mrs. Borrodaile supposed that she had been ill-treated by a callous deceiver who had trifled with her affections, got large sums of money out of her and then deserted her. She had still no idea of the monstrous fraud which had been practised on her, and that Lord Ranelagh, except on the one occasion in Madame's shop, had never heard her name.

Six Criminal Women

When the two ladies were admitted to Madame's presence Mrs. Borrodaile said: "When are you going to get me that money Lord Ranelagh owes me?" Madame, it appeared, disdained to answer her. She turned instead to Miss Sutton and said: "Lord Ranelagh has not had any of her money. Her William has had her money and he will not allow her to leave town. He has been walking backwards and forwards outside for the last two hours." The full horror of her situation now overcame the poor creature. The vileness and brutality of Madame Rachel was at last plain. She stated, and maintained afterwards, that Mrs. Borrodaile was a lustful woman, who, incapable of gratifying herself in any other way, paid a man known as William to meet her on Madame's premises.

Suffering and destitute, Mrs. Borrodaile had reached the nadir of her misfortunes, but help was at hand, though it was not the kind she would have chosen. Her relations had become uneasy about her, and her brother-in-law, Mr. Alfred Cope, had tried to find out what was happening to her and had consulted his solicitors, Messrs. Lewis and Lewis. This news reached Madame Rachel through Mrs. Borrodaile, and one of the last letters from his lordship had warned Mrs. Borrodaile to keep clear of her family's machinations. They would, if allowed their way, inevitably ruin both her honour and the lovers' prospects. "You must write and tell Lewis and Lewis you do not want them to interfere in your affairs or we are betrayed. . . . Cope is at the bottom of all this," added his lordship darkly.

Now that the fiction of Lord Ranelagh was exploded, Mrs. Borrodaile had perforce to let her family have their way. In August 1868 Madame Rachel was brought to trial at the Old Bailey for obtaining money on false pretences.

Two of the three counsel employed for Mrs. Borrodaile, Sergeant Ballantyne and Montagu Williams, have mentioned the trial in their memoirs. Sergeant Ballantyne speaks of

Madame Sarah Rachel Leverson

Madame Rachel as if she had been well known as a procuress, and calls her "one of the most filthy and dangerous moral pests" of the time. Montagu Williams's account is exceptionally interesting, as he gives an abstract of Mrs. Borrodaile's evidence with many details, such as the receipt for the balance of the thousand pounds, of which Mrs. Borrodaile had already paid two hundred before Mr. Haynes sold her stock:

"A receipt for £800, being balance of £1,000, received from me for bath preparations, spices, powders, sponges, perfumes and attendances, to be continued till I am finished by the process." Even more fascinating, both memoirs give a description of Mrs. Borrodaile herself. Ballantyne says: "The quondam beauty, a skeleton encased apparently in plaster of Paris, enamelled pink and white and surmounted with a juvenile wig, tottered into the witness-box." Montagu Williams says: "She had a silly, giggling, half-hysterical way of talking."

The sight did not seem to either of these eminent and experienced men to be anything but ludicrous, and *The Times* report spoke of Mrs. Borrodaile as a "senescent Sappho". It was an era in which the deluded elderly woman who pursued men was a favourite subject of comedy, as can be seen from the number of times such a figure appears in W. S. Gilbert's operas. Our own feelings have become gentler. It is impossible today to read of the scene without pity.

For Mrs. Borrodaile's ordeal was indeed dreadful. Seated on the bench beside the judge, a privileged spectator, was Lord Ranelagh. Montagu Williams says that "During Mrs. Borrodaile's examination he sat with a half-puzzled look upon his face". He cannot be blamed for that, but to hear of the roars of laughter in the court in which he joined gives one the uneasy sensation of being at a gladiatorial show. The defence put forward for Madame Rachel was that she herself had never mentioned Lord Ranelagh to Mrs. Borrodaile; the latter had used the premises in New Bond Street for her assignations, and her money had gone to buy a lover. In support of this theory, Mr. Digby Seymour for Madame Rachel held up to scorn the almost incredible nature of the correspondence.

"Now did Rachel really tell you to write to a nobleman like Lord Ranelagh with instructions that he should get his stockings darned, and buttons put upon his shirts, and that he should send his tattered garments to you to be mended?"

"She did."

Mr. Seymour read out another extract, and then said:

"Now I put you on your solemn oath, did you, when you wrote that letter to this shirtless, buttonless, stockingless, bootless, flannelless, hatless individual, think that you were writing to Lord Ranelagh?"

Amid the shouts of laughter and under Lord Ranelagh's hard stare, Mrs. Borrodaile answered:

"I did. At that time, I had found out he was not a rich man."

There were, among the densely crowded spectators, some who had suffered at Madame Rachel's hands and who gazed at her bold, cruel and opulent figure with concealed feelings of gratification and dread. Madame's composure was unruffled. She seemed perfectly confident of an acquittal, and up to a point her confidence was justified. Sergeant Ballantyne's address to the jury was extremely powerful. He said of the forlorn piece of human wreckage he defended that "Madame Rachel had determined that so long as there were clothes on her back or money at her command, or the possibility of raising it, not a fraction, either in existence or in perspective, should belong to her. . . . There was nothing more to be got out of her. She stood in her clothes. The money and stock were gone. All was swallowed up. . . .

Madame Sarah Rachel Leverson

In the whole category of human wickedness and human folly the equal of this story was undiscoverable."

He carried the feeling of the court with him, but, even so, one member of the jury remained unconvinced, and after an absence of five hours they returned to say they were unable to agree. Madame exclaimed loudly:

"Sensible men!" She added that if they would send their wives to New Bond Street she would beautify them for nothing.

But failure to find a verdict is not the same thing as an acquittal, and Mr. Cope was determined not to let the matter drop. The proceedings were reopened the following month, and this time a verdict of guilty was returned, and Madame Rachel was sentenced to five years' penal servitude.

The strangest part of her story was yet to come. The trial had been fully reported and had received the maximum amount of publicity. Madame Rachel had been so thoroughly discredited that it seemed as if she could never inspire confidence again, and the Magnetic Rock Dew Water itself had come in for rude handling. When Sergeant Ballantyne asked Miss Rachel if she knew where it came from, and she replied, "I knew it came from the East," he had said, "The East might mean Wapping."

In November 1868 an effigy of Madame Rachel was burnt on Guy Fawkes night. Yet, wonderful to relate, when Madame, after four years of her sentence, was released on ticket of leave, in 1872, she reopened her shop, this time more modestly, in Duke Street, Portland Place, and was soon making money, if not quite as fast as before. The governor of Millbank Prison related that she was the only prisoner in his experience who voluntarily returned to the prison precincts. She paid a call on him, dressed in satin, with streaming ostrich feathers.

Once again she proved that she could quietly and steadily

fleece the public, and once again she ruined herself by overweening rapacity.

In 1877, when Madame had been in Portland Place for five lucrative and happy years, a young woman called Mrs. Pearce was attracted by a sign which said "Arabian Perfumer to the Queen" and went in to buy some dentifrice and violet powder. She was a daughter of the famous tenor, Signor Mario; and as one of Madame's daughters, a Mrs. Turner, had been trained as a singer, a sympathetic bond was established. Mrs. Pearce repeated her visit and presently was considering whether she should not be made Beautiful for Ever. "Do you happen to know Lady Dudley?" asked Madame carelessly. When the young client said she did not, Madame said that she had made Lady Dudley Beautiful for Ever at a cost of two thousand pounds. In settlement of the account she had accepted jewels from Lady Dudley to the value of eight thousand pounds, which were in the safe at that moment. Lady Dudley, to conceal the transaction from her family, had given out that the jewels had been stolen at Paddington Station. Mrs. Pearce remembered to have read that Lady Dudley had said so indeed. Of course at the time she had supposed that her ladyship was telling the truth. There was artfulness for you! But the episode naturally invested Madame Rachel with a mysterious grandeur and importance.

However, Mrs. Pearce's resources were slender, and she hesitated to invest in more than a bottle of Jordan Water, which she bought for ten pounds. She applied it, but, so far from any improvements being shown, the terrified client saw a virulent rash coming out on her face. Madame, when consulted, feared that nothing would avail short of the complete beauty treatment. In her great kindness and generosity, she offered this first for one thousand pounds, then for five hundred, and finally for fifty. When her young friend was unable to produce even this paltry sum, she said she would

Madame Sarah Rachel Leverson

make an arrangement like that she had made for Lady Dudley, and accept Mrs. Pearce's jewels instead. Two necklaces were brought, worth about fifty pounds together, and the treatment began.

Meantime, Mrs. Pearce discovered that her necklaces had been pawned at Attenborough's for thirty pounds. Her annoyance and gathering mistrust gave her courage to tell the whole story to her husband, who immediately called in Duke Street and demanded his wife's jewels. Madame refused them with her characteristic truculence, and Mr. Pearce, encouraged no doubt by the success of Mr. Cope before him, sued Madame Rachel for obtaining money by false pretences.

On April 10, 1878, Madame Rachel appeared yet again at the Old Bailey. The trial, after the previous one, was something in the nature of an anticlimax, but it had one feature of extreme interest: it revealed the secrets of Madame's preparations. A young woman called Sabina Pilley was employed by Madame to make up the lotions and prepare the baths, and in the witness-box Miss Pilley said that the Jordan Water came from the pump in the back yard, that the famous washes were composed of water mixed with carbonate of lead, starch, Fuller's earth and hydrochloric acid, and that the Arabian baths were made of hot water and bran. As a result of this trial, Madame received another sentence of five years' penal servitude, but when two of them were over she died in Woking Prison in 1888. There was therefore no opportunity to see whether, after this second exposure, the public would consent to make her fortune for a third time. It seems very likely that they would, however, for with a really remarkable acumen Madame Rachel had discovered and tapped a source that is inexhaustible. That she had been a procuress at some time, and that she was a swindler all the time, are not the interesting features of her career. She is extraordinary because she anticipated by more than half a century the most modern methods of advertising. She and her daughters, as the team who wrote *Beautiful for Ever* and ran the shop, would have had nothing to learn from courses in salesmanship or the findings of Consumer Research. Her unerring detection of the weakness, the fears, the desires, of a great part of humanity, her instinctive perception of how the mind will react under the influence of these feelings, were equalled only by her commercial genius which told her that you can sell pump-water as a precious essence if only you charge enough for it. Madame's successors have made some improvement in the stock in trade, and their manner to a dissatisfied client is more decorous than hers, but a comparison of her professional methods and theirs will give rise to many interesting reflections.

ALICE PERRERS

Extravagance and greed—the desire to spend money or to hoard it—are accepted as natural qualities in a king's mistress. To have the king of England or the king of France for a lover placed such glittering temptation in a woman's way she could scarcely be blamed for yielding to it. Not only was she given absolute power to take what she liked, but some of the finest things in the world were there for her to choose: houses, furniture, pictures, ornaments, china, plate, jewels, and each object so beautiful of its kind that we of the mass-production age can see its like only in a musuem. If we honestly ask ourselves what our own degree of self-restraint would have been if we had been able to rifle the palaces of Charles II or George IV, we cannot be surprised at the almost universal covetousness of royal mistresses. Two of the very few who escaped this charge were Louise de la Valliere and Nell Gwynne. Louise de la Valliere, drawn into a liaison against her will, wanted nothing from Louis XIV; and though Nell Gwynne received a great deal of money, her hearty affection for Charles absolved her from the charge of self-seeking.

To a very large extent the public are prepared to regard the acquisitions of a king's mistress as lawful perquisites. It takes an unusual degree of covetousness in such a woman for her to be regarded as an evil-doer because of it, but this rare distinction was gained by the mistress of Edward III. Not only was the greed of Alice Perrers monstrous, but the means she took to satisfy it remove her from the ranks of the merely expensive and put her definitely among the criminal.

Six Criminal Women

Edward III's marriage had been a particularly happy one, worthy to compare with that of Queen Victoria. He had married at sixteen the fourteen-year-old French countess, Philippa of Hainault, whom, child as she was, he had already loved for some years. He had known that she loved him, because she cried when he left her mother's court after a visit. Edward had finished a victorious expedition against the Scots and was still in the north when Philippa landed at Dover. Froissart says: "The young queen and her menie journeyed north until they came to York, where she was received with great solemnity. And all the lords of England who were in the city came forth in fair array to meet her, and with them the young king mounted on an excellently paced hackney, magnificently clad and arrayed; and he took her by the hand and embraced and kissed her; and so, riding side by side, with great plenty of minstrels and honours, they entered the city." The wedding was held in York Minster in 1327, their son the Black Prince was born the following year, and after him six other sons and five daughters.

The splendid physique of the young father—tall, powerful and debonair—was handed on to the sons, but not his charming nature. A rhyming chronicle says:

> *So high and large they were of all stature*
> *The least of them was of his person able*
> *To have foughten with any creature,*

but with the exception of the Black Prince, who was admired for his chivalry in the whole of Europe, they were a disagreeable brood, violent, selfish and incapable. The worst was unfortunately the one who took most part in public affairs, John Duke of Lancaster, called Gaunt because he was born in Ghent when his mother was visiting her relations.

Edward himself was one of the first of the great English

Alice Perrers

kings, and his long reign covered a period of such intense development of the national genius and the national life as was not seen again until the age of Elizabeth. The civilised but vigorous daily existence is shown most clearly of all in Chaucer's poetry, but we can see it from another angle in the illuminations of the time, such as the wonderful series of pictures illustrating Froissart's chronicle, a few years after Edward's death. These remind us of the imaginative readjustment we must make in evoking the London of the late fourteenth century; that, for instance, the stone buildings, such as the Tower, the Abbey and Westminster Hall, which the Londoner sees as characteristically grey, were then newly built, ungrimed by centuries of smoke, and of a dazzling white. Trees and grass of an emerald freshness, such as we see only in the country, were all about the city inside and out. King Arthur's court was described as "going a-maying in the woods and fields beside Westminster", and Saffron Hill in the city is so called because the monks used to grow sheets of crocuses there for the manufacture of yellow dye. The Thames was a transparent, sparkling river running on gravel reaches; the poet Dunbar said its waters were like beryl, a blue-green translucent stone, and that swans and barges swam on it. He also spoke of the white pillars of London Bridge that spanned it, on which he saw merchants walking up and down, and knights in velvet gowns with chains of gold. The brightness, clarity and freshness of the scene was equalled in degree by the filth and horrors on the ground itself. In the reign succeeding Edward III's, the earliest Urban Sanitary Act forbade the casting of all "Annoyances, Dung, Garbage, Entrails and other Ordure, in ditches, rivers and waters", and ordered such refuse to be utterly removed and carried away out of the streets. The same contrast was experienced in the great houses, where the spare, spiritual beauty of Gothic architecture rose airily over whole communities living without sanitation, robes sewn all over with jewels dragged across floors strewn with rushes, matted with the filth of months, and men ate meat with their fingers out of gold and silver dishes and threw the bones to the dogs under the table.

In his prime, Edward was a personal manifestation of the national genius. The nation for the first time gained enormous prestige by his victories in the French War, which had for a time the effect of making France, the greatest and most civilised nation of the world, a province of England, the unknown, mist-shrouded island with a population of some two million people. The Plantagenet cast of face is very distinctive, and it descended even to the weak and decadent Richard II. Its characteristic features are eyebrows springing in a curve high above eyes that are heavily lidded, and a long, straight nose with wide-flaring nostrils. Edward's curling hair and beard were blonde and this enhanced his debonair appearance. Froissart says that anyone who thought suddenly of the king's face, or dreamed of it, took this as a presage of good luck. He was of an extremely well-balanced nature, courageous and firm, high-spirited and gentle, affectionate and of great generosity. It has been suggested that the famous episode in which Queen Philippa, great with child, knelt before him and begged the lives of the burghers of Calais, was arranged by him to do honour to the queen's gentleness and her power over him; since it is thought impossible that a man of Edward's well-known decency would have intended to put the men to death in any case. If this be so, it emphasizes his cast of mind even more strongly than if the whole had been spontaneous. The incident is rather less pleasing viewed as a coup de théatre, but it shows what ceremonial honour he liked to pay to gentleness and mercy.

There is only one recorded instance of Edward's falling in love with another woman during the queen's lifetime, and this, according to Froissart, took place when Edward

Alice Perrers

was thirty-one. He had gone north to relieve Wark Castle from the Scots, and was received in her husband's absence by the lovely Countess of Salisbury, who is supposed to be the original of the lady in the Garter legend. Froissart says of Edward: "He was stricken therewith to the heart with a sparkle of fine love that endured long after. He thought no lady in the world so worthy to be loved as she."

Apart from this passion, which was never gratified, it would seem that the queen had little cause for jealousy. She had at least no serious rival in the king's affection. Two years before her death, however, which occurred in 1369 when the queen was fifty-six, he had at least noticed one of her waiting women. He had given the lady a grant of two tuns yearly of Gascon wine. Edward was a man who gave many presents, and Alice Perrers may have been one among several ladies of the household to receive the king's gifts; but on the queen's death Alice's position became at once defined. It was not many months before she was known all over Europe as the English king's concubine.

There has been a strange attempt on the part of some writers to prove that Alice Perrers was of high lineage, a lady "of sense and merit", whose innocent friendship with the king was owing to her agreeable conversation. It is true that if trifling alterations are made in her Christian name and her surname, a choice of respectable origins may be claimed for her. If Alice be changed to Elizabeth, she could be the daughter of John and Gunnora Perrers, of Holt in Norfolk. If Perrers be read "Perrot" she could be the niece of William of Wykeham himself. But the other claim is untenable in any circumstances. Sense, merit and agreeable conversation are very pleasant qualities in themselves, but even supposing Alice to have had all three, they would not account for her extraordinary ascendancy over the king, and for the staggering amount of property which it procured for her. Something else is required to arouse sexual passion, and only violent sexual passion will put such a man so completely in the power of such a woman.

The earliest account of her says that she was of low origin. This is a seventeenth-century translation of a chronicle called *An Historical Relation of certain Passages about the End of Edward III*. The Latin original was presumably written soon after the king's death, as it mentions the death of the Black Prince as a recent event and speaks of John of Gaunt in the present tense. The writer is clearly hostile to Alice Perrers, and one has to bear this in mind in accepting his verdicts, but his assertion that she was a weaver's daughter of the town of Hunaye ("beside Exeter, as some suppose") commends itself to the modern reader; obscure birth is no reproach to our way of thinking, and she is the more interesting if her native ability raised her from the proletariat. Furthermore, her abnormal rapacity suggests a person who had known want.

The chronicler says "she learned the ways of love" from a fool who used to carry water from a conduit to private houses. How she managed with these antecedents to gain a footing in court circles, in any capacity, is not explained, but it is clear that once her foot was inside the door her success would be immediate and complete. The writer says that she was "neither beautiful nor fair", but nor was Cleopatra. Sexual magnetism can exist quite independently of beauty. Even he admits the charm of her way of speech.

Edward III was fifty-eight when Philippa died. The expectation of life in the Middle Ages was little more than forty, and his complete subjugation by Alice Perrers was regarded by his horrified contemporaries as a symptom of dotage. It is difficult for us with our completely different scale of ages to view the king's passion in this light, but it is a matter of common experience that elderly men may become infatuated with women much younger than themselves. Edward had lost the dear companion of over forty years,

Alice Perrers

and thus was particularly susceptible to the charm of a woman who made him forget that he was lonely and old. He had once delighted to show that he could refuse nothing to his queen, and now he found a pleasure in yielding to the requests of Alice Perrers.

Alice began immediately to turn his infatuation to account. The short lives of many parents meant that their children were orphaned while minors. Their guardianship was frequently bestowed by the king on some favourite who drew the income from their estate in return for his protection, and exacted a heavy sum on the ward's marriage. Robert de Tiliol, John Payne and Richard Lord Poynings were three young unfortunates who fell at once into Alice's net. Whenever an estate was left without an heir, or was otherwise forfeit to the Crown, Alice obtained it simply for the asking. In the year of Philippa's death, the king's aunt also died, and her manor, some open fields, a forest and a piece of land were all made over to the favourite. In Essex alone she acquired the manors of Upminster, Bradwell, Hokkale, Pilton, Daneseye, West Newland and Steple, and within a short time she was owning properties in sixteen other counties, from Northumberland to Devon.

The monastery of St. Albans in Hertfordshire were powerful landowners. A pious woman, Joanna Whitewell, left them at her death her manor of Oxhey, and the abbot at once took possession of it and put in tenants. There had, however, been a legal dispute between Joanna Whitewell and her neighbour Thomas FitzJohn, who now asserted that that manor belonged to him; and coming with his retainers, he evicted the abbot's tenants. The people on the estate, however, were quite clear that they preferred the monks as landlords to the private owner, and they joined with the abbot's men in resisting FitzJohn. The resistance was so formidable that he abandoned the attack and went to work in another direction.

Six Criminal Women

He went to London and saw Alice Perrers, and for a consideration he conveyed Oxhey manor to her, departing with his settlement and leaving her to make her claim good. Alice at once sent down her seneschal, Robert of Warwick, to take possession. The seneschal convened the reluctant tenants to take oaths to their lady, who was known from one shire's end to another as the most merciless of rapacious landlords. But her reputation had other aspects as well. Not only had Thomas FitzJohn, unable to get the better of the abbot of St. Albans, gone to her at once as the champion against all comers, but the abbot himself, once Alice was installed, recognized that it would be useless to contest with her. The monks tacitly relinquished their claim. It was not until many years later, when her power was gone, that they turned her men off the manor and resumed the property.

The king's passion became a theme of national indignation and dismay. It was recognized that there were no bounds to Alice's influence. "She so bewitched him that he permitted the wars and the greatest matters of the realm to be defined by her council." The reference to the wars perhaps concerns the incident of 1372 when Edward, accompanied by the Black Prince, embarked with an expedition to attack Thouars. The company took ship at Sandwich, but the wind was contrary, and after waiting on it for some time the King disembarked. No sooner had he done so than it veered again and the Black Prince expected to put out immediately. To the scandal of all, Edward paid no attention to the now favourable wind but countermanded the expedition and returned at once to London and to Alice Perrers. It was said that the wasted preparations had cost nine hundred thousand pounds.

Among other sources of revenue Alice found that she could exploit her influence in the law courts. "Her dishonest malapertness increased so much" that when a cause

Alice Perrers

in which she was financially interested was being heard Alice would appear in Westminster Hall and seat herself on the bench beside the judge. This example of the insolence of power has perhaps never been surpassed. From this vantage ground, Alice instructed the judge in what verdict he ought to give. "The judges who, fearing the king's displeasure, or rather, more truly, fearing the harlot's, durst not oftentimes judge otherwise than she had defined." Alice was in fact perpetrating the crime of "Maintainance". It was known that she would use her influence to secure a favourable verdict for a suitor provided she were given a sufficiently large share of the gains. Thus it was said of her that she would "defend false causes everywhere by unlawful means, to get possession for her own use".

She also worked in a combine. Lord Latymer, the English governor of Becherel, and a wealthy merchant, Richard Lyons, were in an extremely profitable partnership. Latymer was in a position to know what imports were bound for the English ports. Lyons, acting on his information, made a "corner" in them. Alice was admitted to the partnership, because if legal difficulties should arise it was useful to have a confederate whose mere word to the king would secure a free pardon. Lord Latymer found this line of business so profitable that "he filled barrels with gold and sent them to his own places". Richard Lyons, as the man who acted on the information, must have made even more, and though the accounts are not produced it must be fairly safe to say that whatever the gentlemen's share the lady would not have been satisfied with anything less. Between them, it was said: "They have made such a great scarcity in the land of things saleable that the common people can scarce live."

Another branch of the combine's activities depended not on their own astuteness, but solely on the mistress's power over the king. Edward III had many creditors. Alice and

Six Criminal Women

her two associates approached them and offered to take over the debts for a cash settlement at considerably less than the original amount. The creditors were glad to compound. Alice then presented the demands to the Treasury in her own name and received a payment in full.

Alice's own private depredations went on unceasingly. The king gave her of his own will rich and valuable presents, but even the kingly bounty of the lover could not keep pace with the rapacity of the mistress. Whatever he might give her, she was always beforehand with him, wanting something else. She was one of the daughters of the horse-leech, crying, Give! Give! The king gave her the jewels that had belonged to the late queen, a present so magnificent in itself and of such significance that it might have stopped her mouth. But, quite the contrary, she helped herself to more gems and ornaments from the Treasury, and the Treasury accounts show, opposite the name of Dame Ales Perrers, "a pardon of the value of the jewels she had of us". Some of them she afterwards sold the king again. As the Fool said: "Pleasure will be paid, one time or another."

Alice owned a great deal of house property, not only on her estates in the seventeen counties, but in the City of London, where she built several "in the Ropery, between Weston Lane and Wolfy Lane". The one she lived in herself when she was not in the king's palace at Westminster or Havering or Sheen or Eltham, was at Hammersmith, a moated manor called Pallenswick. This was the home of the two little girls she bore to Edward, who appear in her will as Joan and Joan, but whose names should perhaps be read as Joan and Jane. To furnish this home, Alice plundered the royal wardrobe like an English soldier let loose among the houses of the French. The officials could not prevent her taking whatever struck her fancy, but, unknown to her, an ominous situation developed. Every time she took something they wrote it down. To a certain extent this was

Alice Perrers

natural and simply a part of their duties. When Alice removed wholesale consignments of bedding, carpets, clothes and plate, the officials responsible for their custody would be expected to make a note of the fact. But the meticulous accuracy with which every single item was listed, including a remnant of linen cloth and a yard of ribbon, suggests a personal hatred rather than mere book-keeping. When her day was in eclipse these lists, containing scores upon scores of articles, were produced with orders to the sheriffs of London to see that the property was returned to Sir Alan Stokes, the keeper of the wardrobe.

The lists are of fascinating interest in themselves, but to assess their value by anything like modern standards one must remember not only that money was about forty times as valuable in the fourteenth century as it is today, but that the intrinsic value of objects was immeasurable by any scale of ours. Each object of domestic use in Edward's palace—each spoon, each girdle, each counterpane—was a costly work of art; but not only that, it was precious not only as a beautiful object but because it was a useful one. In the reign of Edward III the scantiness of personal and domestic possessions, even in the families of the great, strikes us with amazement. The household furniture of one of the wealthiest citizens of Colchester at the end of the fourteenth century was inventoried for taxation purposes as follows: a trestle table, two silver spoons, a cup, a tablecloth, two towels, a brass cauldron, a brass dish, washing-basin and ewer, trivet and iron candlestick, two beds, two gowns, one mantle, and was valued at two pounds, five shillings and fivepence.[1] This helps one to realize that though the lists of Alice Perrers's thefts even in their entirety might not strike one as so very outrageous in the circumstances, they did in fact represent an absolute orgy of looting. Among the most interesting things she took were furnishings for her bed. These included

[1] *Mediaeval Panorama*, G. G. Coulton, C.u.p.

Six Criminal Women

curtains and canopy of white satin, rayed with gold, with gold cords, a mattress, feather bed, and bolster, four pillows covered with linen cloth, two sheets, two blankets of white worsted, a covering of white silk and a valance of white tapestry "powdered with boterflies". She had three curtains of red taffeta, three of white taffeta, three of green taffeta and three of green woollen "wrought with chaplets of roses", six white tapestry carpets, a large iron-bound coffer lined with cloth, and a long trestle table. She took twelve silver basins, two little gilt basins, six silver spoons, one gilt spice dish, one gilt salt, two silver lanterns, two baskets covered with velvet and tied with silver.

Among clothes and ornaments taken by her were twenty-two buttons with eagles, one chaplet of pearls, one collar of silver (broken), four gold buttons, a pair of gloves embroidered with daisies, a yellow cap, a white mantle, five yards of damask ribbon and two collars for little dogs "with silver cokkebelles".

The most interesting mention of her clothes, however, comes, not from the lists of her appropriations, but from the proper Wardrobe accounts, and are notes of garments made for her and given to her. In 1376 one of the greatest of the mediaeval tournaments was held in Smithfield. It was a spectacular demonstration of the power and influence of the weaver's daughter. Edward's reign was an era when the enthusiasm for tournaments was at its height, but this one made so much impression that it is the only one particularly noted in the chronicles of the time except one of similar splendour held in Queen Philippa's youth, when the ladies' stand collapsed and only the queen's personal intervention saved the carpenters from dire punishment.

No such mishap marred the present occasion. Alice, as queen of the lists, was called the Lady of the Sun. Her retinue consisted of lords on horseback, each of whom was led by a lady: a graceful repetition of the central theme

Alice Perrers

which was supplied by Alice, seated in a chariot beside the enchanted king. The Chronicle of London from 1089-1483 says: "In this year rode Dame Alice Perrers as Lady of the Sun fro the Tour of London through Chepeside, and alway a lady leading a lordy's brydelle. And then began the grete justes in Smithfield which endured vii daies." Alice's clothes supplied by the wardrobe for this occasion were: a russet gown lined with white cloth and a cap of tanned kid leather broidered with gold thread and bound with gold ribbon, furred with ermine.

Women's dress of the time was very charming, with a small, high-waisted bodice and long, full skirt, and sleeves tight to the wrist with a loose, elbow sleeve about them, hanging almost to the ground. The bodice was sometimes off the shoulders and trimmed with fur. The beautiful effect of bare shoulders, rising from a band of ermine, over a scarlet or sapphire dress, is a familiar sight in the illuminations. The lining of a gown, so often mentioned, was important; it showed not only in the long upper sleeves, but sometimes the skirt was pulled up through the girdle in front, revealing the underskirt and its own lining in the folds.

Another Smithfield tournament was planned to repeat the success of the first, and Alice's clothes were to be still more resplendent. This time the wardrobe produced a cloth of gold tissue lined with red and white taffeta. The second tournament never took place, however, as the Black Prince died on the eve of Pentecost, but no doubt Alice made occasions to wear the gold dress, notwithstanding.

Other gowns she had from the wardrobe were: a scarlet gown furred with minever, with a hood, a sanguine cloak furred with squirrel, a sanguine gown and hood furred with minever.

Another fashion was of silk or satin clothes sewn all over with jewels. The anonymous poem "Pearl" describes the heroine in a white satin dress sewn with pearls at hems and wristbands, "at sides, at openings", and a kirtle covered with pearl embroidery. The gems used for this work were of the less valuable kinds. The "Scots" pearls, for instance, were thought suitable only for embroidery, or for great church ornaments where a massed effect was wanted. Alice, needless to say, took great quantities of gems for her clothes, all of which were counted and priced by the indefatigable wardrobe men. Part of the account against her runs: five hundred pearls each at one and eightpence, seventeen thousand pearls at tenpence, five thousand, nine hundred and forty precious stones at fivepence, two thousand precious stones at fourpence, three thousand, nine hundred and forty-eight precious stones at threepence, and thirty ounces of pearls valued in gross at fifty pounds. If the prices are multiplied by forty, the value even of the embroidery stones is not trivial.

Alice's splendid appearance matched with her ruthless greed made her a figure of national detestation. Her scarlet robes and gold ribbons, her ermine and her gems, made a challenging target for violent hostility. In a land whose population was less than that of London today, it was possible for a state of feeling to sweep the entire nation. The unpopularity of Alice raged high and low through every walk of life. One arresting sign of this, among many, was the incident of the sailors. Alice had some quarrel whose origin is unknown with a sailor on board one of the king's ships, and settled it by having him assassinated by a squire of her own retinue. At this time John of Gaunt was acting as regent because the king was failing and the Black Prince invalided by malaria. "About Aester the duke caused the whole navy to be gathered together at London, but why he did so, he only knoweth." Nevertheless, there they all were, when the murderer of their companion was brought to trial. It was rumoured among the mob that the trial was not being conducted in any serious manner because the justices knew

Alice Perrers

that Alice Perrers had already provided herself with a free pardon, to be produced if the verdict went against her squire. When the sailors heard this, "with a furious madness they run into the house" where the murderer was detained. They dragged him out and "killed him like a swine with a knife" and hung the corpse on the nearest gallows. Then, "as though they had done a great act, they caused the trumpeters to go before them unto the ships, where, in great mirth, they spent the rest of the day".

When the authorities attempted to rebuke them, the sailors made this reply: "That the king now had great need of their help who, if he would not pardon them, they would depart from him and seek such a man that both should know how to keep them and also would love them, and with a strong hand would oppose those that wrought them any evil."

The episode in itself probably weighed little with Alice. Her victim was dead, and her instrument would not be able to give her any trouble in the future. "Stone dead hath no fellow." But as a demonstration against herself its significance was not lost on her.

Indeed the drawback to her position was that she had confederates, but no friend. Her power and wealth were enormous, but they rested on the life of one ailing old man, and when he expired the structure of her fortune might tumble and dissolve like a sand castle under the incoming waves. It may have been this feeling of insecurity which led her to take up with Sir William de Windsor, a wellborn but somewhat battered and needy knight, who had served the king's son Lionel of Clarence in the government of Ireland. She may also have seen in her new relationship a hitherto untapped source of profit. She may even have liked Sir William for his own sake. If she did, she must afterwards have blamed herself severely for having allowed pleasure to interfere with business.

Six Criminal Women

The Duke of Clarence was an early example of the Englishman completely routed by the Irish. When he left the country, saying that nothing should induce him ever to set foot in it again, he left de Windsor behind him as Lord Lieutenant. It hardly looks like coincidence that de Windsor's career of brutal extortion in Ireland was coeval with his friendship with Alice at home. While Edward III was still on his feet, he tried to check de Windsor's abuse of government. He forbade him to collect the grants which de Windsor had forced the Dubliners to vote him, and he appointed more than one public inquiry under Sir Nicholas Dagworth into the Lieutenant's very dubious methods. But the king was now too feeble to assert himself. He saw the outside world through a distorting glass that Alice perpetually held up to him. Her wish was law. The sum of eleven thousand pounds was ordered to be paid to de Windsor, and part of his obligation in return was to provide and maintain two hundred soldiers and forty archers for the Irish service. The money was paid out by the Treasury—but it was paid to Alice Perrers. Of wages, the two hundred and forty soldiers never received a penny. Like will to like, and while their interests remained the same, the relationship of Sir William and Dame Alice must have been exquisitely harmonious.

In 1376, one year before the king's death, it became necessary to summon a parliament that money might be voted to carry on the government. This assembly which became known as the Good Parliament, to the astonishment of all except those who had had private word beforehand, opened with a burst of denunciation of some of the most highly placed persons in the kingdom. John of Gaunt was severely criticized, by implication at least, for his incompetence as Regent; Lord Latymer was declared "unprofitable to the king and the realm" and relieved of his office; and Richard Lyons was to be imprisoned during the king's

Alice Perrers

pleasure. Finally, and most remarkable of all, Alice Perrers was brought to book.

A formidable body of accusation had been prepared in secret. The knights of the seventeen shires in which her properties lay each told a tale of extortionate oppression. She was accused of "maintaining" cases in the law courts, and her influence over the king was said to have brought the country into ignominy and failure. It is extraordinarily interesting to notice that, side by side with so much grave and penetrating censure, these capable men placed an accusation of black magic. The ascendancy of Alice Perrers over the greatest king in Christendom seemed to them impossible to account for by normal means. They singled out a Dominican friar who formed part of her household at Pallenswick and said that under his guidance she had bewitched the king: "allured him to her unlawful love", says the chronicler, "or as I may trulyer say, into madness". The Commons alleged that the friar made, "as they say Moses did in times past, rings of memory and forgetfulness", and so worked with spells that she was never out of the king's mind.

The Dominican, as well as being a physician, had a touch of clairvoyance, and it is quite probable that Alice bought his spells. Neither he nor she nor the Commons themselves would seem to have understood that the most potent spell was her own.

While these matters were being expounded at Westminster, two members, Sir John Delamere and Sir John Brentwood, rode out to Hammersmith to secure the friar. Inspecting the patient's water was a favourite method of diagnosis of the time and the knights rode into the courtyard with urinals in their hands, pretending that they had come for professional advice. The friar was standing at an upper window, and when he saw them appear with these instruments he came down to receive the supposed patients.

47

The knights at once took him into custody and prepared to ride off with him. A servant girl who stood by asked the friar why he had not been able to foresee this. He replied that he had foreseen a parliament during which he and his mistress should meet with great reverses, but he had not known when it was to be.

He was examined by the Commons for the greater part of the day, and the proceedings against him were ended by the Archbishop of Canterbury's suggestion that he should be returned to the control of his Order. The archbishop, Simon Sudbury, was famous for his mild and compassionate judgments and was sometimes blamed for them. In Richard II's reign the rebels killed him on Tower Hill.

Meanwhile the knights proclaimed that Alice was deeply in love with Sir William de Windsor, which may possibly have been true, however unlikely, and added that she was married to him, which at this time was certainly untrue. A body of them waited on the king and explained to him that his mistress was married and that he had therefore been living in adultery. Edward, with his old firmness and good sense, refused to believe them. So strong, however, did the Commons feel themselves that they were able to impose their will upon him. They forced him to promise that he would relinquish his amour. The archbishop's cross was held out for him to kiss, and with this solemn action he vowed never to see Alice Perrers again. In the famous passage of his *Life of Chaucer* Godwin says: "It was barbarous to dictate in this unfeeling manner to a monarch who had once been the arbiter of Europe, and to tear from the aged prince, now in his sixty-fifth year, a companion and confidant whom habit had rendered necessary to him." There is much to be said for this view; and had Alice Perrers been anything other than what she was, it would no doubt have been taken by Parliament itself. The chronicler says that Alice had long been borne with by an angry people because of their love to

Alice Perrers

the king. "For there is in them (the English) a special grace, that they love their king more than any other nation, and whom they have once admitted to the kingly state, they always honour though he greatly offend." But Alice appeared to them less a woman than a devouring pestilence, and when they had an opportunity to get rid of her it was too much to hope that they would not make the fullest use of it. Alice's estates were forfeit and she was banished from the court, on pain of excommunication if she returned.

The inspiration of the Good Parliament had been the Black Prince, who, prostrated by bouts of the malaria he had contracted in Spain, lived as a complete invalid in his house at Berkhampstead. This unfortunate sickness removed from the political sphere Edward III's immediate heir, his only good and capable son and the most famous knight in the chivalry of Europe. It opened the door to the disreputable John of Gaunt, and ultimately meant that Edward III was succeeded by his grandson Richard, a child of ten years old. Laid up as the Black Prince was, he was still the mainspring of the party that detested his brother. One of the thrusts which the Speaker of the Good Parliament made at John of Gaunt was to affirm that the succession was provided for in the young Prince Richard if his father were to die an early death. This death occurred while Parliament still sat. "The same season, on Trinity Sunday, there passed out of this world the flower of chivalry of England, Edward Prince of Wales and Aquitaine, at the king's palace of Westminster beside London." The effect upon the party which had been supported by his influence was like that of pulling the string out of a row of beads. The Parliament was dissolved once it had voted the necessary money, and its edicts were blown away after it. Alice Perrers returned to the king.

The threat of excommunication remained idle. "The Archbishop and his suffragans, like dumb dogs, not able to bark." Alice's influence was all-powerful as before. The king had been miserably unhappy in her absence, and was failing fast. Alice's company restored him to cheerfulness, and she would not let him dwell on approaching death. Her conversation was all upon "hunting and hawking" and the pleasures of this world. She immediately secured the return of her estates. They had been given to the king's sons and a mandate from their father obliged the disappointed princes to give them up. Her influence next turned in another direction, by no means purely disinterested, though exerted on behalf of somebody else. John of Gaunt had persuaded the king to appoint Sir Nicholas Dagworth once more to inquire into de Windsor's misgovernment of Ireland. The overweening insolence of Alice had by no means abated during her banishment, and, furious at this move against her confederate, she prepared on her own responsibility a document commanding Sir Nicholas Dagworth's recall. John of Gaunt was about to leave London and he had his last interview with the king on this subject at the king's bedside, for Edward did not leave his bed. As Gaunt left the bedchamber he met Alice at the door, who condescended to plead with him that Sir Nicholas might not be sent. Gaunt answered haughtily that it was the king's will. But he was leaving the king's chamber and Alice was coming into it. The next morning he came to the king's bedside to say goodbye and was told that the king had decided to cancel Sir Nicholas Dagworth's appointment.

One more suit Alice managed to secure, before death defeated her. William of Wykham, the bishop of Winchester, had incurred the hostility of John of Gaunt. As one stands at the west door of Winchester Cathedral and looks up the nave whose astounding beauty is his memorial, it is difficult to think of the man who devised this almost supernatural effect of height and grace: who carved thick Norman pillars into clusters of three slender shafts, who removed a flat ceiling and put in airy fan vaulting, and lowered plinths

Alice Perrers

so that at a little distance the pillars seem to spring from the floor itself, and repeated these effects down a vista of the longest nave in England, to think of such a man as involved in a worldly and sordid dispute, accused of malversation of funds, taking fines from hostages and cheating the crown. So deeply had he offended the regent, however, that when a general pardon was extended to malefactors to celebrate the king's jubilee William of Wykham was excepted by name. The result was that, though his spiritual office remained, his temporal possessions were confiscated to the crown.

The king was plainly about to die, and it was possible that he might be succeeded by the bishop's inveterate enemy, Gaunt. A desperate expedient was called for and there was no time to lose. The bishop approached Alice Perrers and asked her to name her price for persuading the king to restore him his temporalities. Alice agreed. What she demanded is not known, but she induced the king, within three days of his death, to restore the bishop's lands.

And now she could see that her reign was counted by hours only. The shorter the time that remained the more precious it was. She sat by the king's pillow all day and lay in his bed all night. No one could have a private word with him. She diverted his last thoughts from his family and friends, and from making any provision for his old servants. The chronicler says in these last hours she sat by him "much like a dog that waited greedily to snatch whatsoever his master would throw under the board, so she with greedy chaps and wide gaping and uncomely grinning, still waited if anything might fall". She had received the king's provision for her two daughters, and one of the last morsels she was able to snatch for herself was the renewal of the old grant for two tuns yearly of Gascon wine.

Her greed had done for her what the ruling passion always does: it had destroyed all sense of proportion. When she saw that death was stealing over him, "she took the rings from his fingers which for his royal majesty he was wont to wear", and stole quietly away, leaving the dying man alone in an empty room. She had done worse things, but nothing that showed such an utter lack of the qualities that ordinary men and women expect from their fellow beings. This is the action that is always connected with her name.

The king, however, did not die alone. One of the household chaplains passing the entrance to the bed chamber saw to his astonishment that the dying man was unattended. He came up to the bed, "inwardly touched with grief that among so many councillors which he had had, there was none who would say unto him the words of life". The kind and humble priest bent over the king and spoke to him as "Loving lord". He asked him to think about his sins and to ask God's mercy on them. The king had strength only for one word. He said, "Jesus." "By and by he took the cross in his hands, and with tears and sighing, he put it to his mouth; and within a little while after he yielded his spirit unto God."

Alice had been right when she foresaw that there was no future for her after the king's death. She had expected that she would have to make do with what she already had. Besides the landed property in seventeen counties, the house property in London, and the wealth in kind, she had, it was said, twenty thousand pounds, or, by our estimate, eight hundred thousand pounds. What she had not reckoned upon, despite her knowledge of her own unpopularity which was betrayed in the indecent haste with which she had left the king, was that the government had marked her down for immediate retribution. The first parliament of the young Richard II reaffirmed her banishment and that her estates were forfeit. It was the estates which Gaunt was particularly anxious to see reclaimed, but at the same time an order was made for the return of various crown jewels, and now the

Alice Perrers

lists of the wardrobe officials were brought out. How much of this property was recovered must be doubtful. Sheets and pillows and yards of ribbon would not be easy to trace in someone else's house, but at least the hostile intention of the government was clear.

Alice was never reduced to poverty. Indeed, judging from the condition in which she began her life, she ended it in prosperity, but for the time between 1369 and 1377, the eight years of almost unbelievable good fortune, she paid with twenty-three remaining years of ceaseless disappointment, anxiety and restless care. It was retribution of the justest kind. If she had been content to take her money and retire with her daughters to Pallenswick, giving up the crown jewels and allowing her other property to go where it would, she could have enjoyed twenty years as a comfortable and prosperous elderly woman. But her riches had such a hold over her that she could not see any other object in life except the attempt to get them back. For twenty years she pleaded and petitioned, she quarrelled privately and went to law, and the worst taste of bitterness was infused by someone whom she had never expected to betray her.

As she was a banished person, she had not the right to petition parliament. For this reason, or perhaps for this among others, she married William de Windsor, and he undertook to plead her cause. He did it with such success that a grant was made, restoring his wife's property to him. In December 1379 her sentence of banishment was repealed; it seemed, therefore, that the worst of Alice's troubles were over, but they had in fact only begun. De Windsor was made Governor of Cherbourg, and was therefore absent from his wife for most of the year. This made it possible for him to keep to himself a very important piece of information, which he could scarcely have withheld from so astute a woman had they been continually together. De Windsor died in 1384, and Alice then discovered that by the terms of the grant the estates did not revert to her, but to her husband's heir, his nephew, John de Windsor. The fury of Alice was indescribable, and it consumed her for the rest of her life. For twelve miserable years she pursued John de Windsor. Whenever parliament met, and wherever it was convened, at Westminster, Oxford, Winchester or Shrewsbury, the ageing virago appeared, spectre-like, with her tale of grievances that the pressure of new affairs was pushing farther and farther away in the memories of men. She was sometimes listened to, sometimes she was promised redress, but the promise was never kept. Hamlet mentioned the law's delays as one of the causes that might drive men to suicide, and Alice experienced this torment to the full, though her hardy and bellicose temperament would never have allowed her to put such an end to the struggle.

She died at last in her manor of Upminster which she had been allowed to keep. Both her daughters were married, and she left to them the lands for whose possession she had embittered so much of her life, but neither of them cared to carry on the useless attempt.

It is impossible to say how old she was at any of the periods of her life; but supposing that she had captivated the king when she was twenty (though she might well have been much less), she would have been just over fifty when she died. Her will was proved in February 1401.

The strange thing about Alice Perrers is that on the one hand she bewitched King Edward so entirely and that on the other she seems to have attracted nobody else. With the dubious exception of William de Windsor, she would seem to have had no admirers other than the king. Lovers one would not expect her to have had: she was too single-minded in her pursuit of wealth to have risked her position in such a way. But she seems to have had for men in general none of that charm which can overcome hostility by personal contact, such as Mary Stuart had, for example. That she had

Alice Perrers

remarkable strength of character is obvious, but strong-minded women are not usually the ones attractive to men. Yet the king's dependence on her was owing partly at least to a real enjoyment of her society. He was not simply dominated by an overbearing woman whom he couldn't shake off. He was genuinely happy in her company. When he was too frail to leave his bed, her return brought him back a zest for existence. Within a few days of his death, her talking to him of hunting and hawking made him think that he might ride out once again. Spells and charms, and rings of memory and forgetfulness, were called in to explain this miracle of nature.

The strongest denunciation of Alice Perrers and her greed is so majestic that it is almost a tribute. Langland in his *Vision of Piers Plowman,* devotes two of his visions to the Lady Mede. The word Mede, or reward, is used to cover the whole conception of money put to base uses, and the poem illustrates with its wonderful wealth of detail the power of bribery and corruption in Church and State. The personification of Mede as a rich woman has always been understood to be a picture of Alice Perrers. The symbolism expresses, beside the larger issues, exactly what was felt about her, and some of the details of appearance repeat with peculiar accuracy what we know of her.

The writer says that on looking to his left hand, in the Field full of Folk, he was

> Ware of a woman, wonderly clad,
> Her robe, fur edged, the finest on earth.
> Crowned with a crown, the king hath no better.
> Fairly her fingers were fretted with rings,
> And in the rings red rubies as red as a furnace.
> And diamonds of dearest price and double sapphires,
> Sapphires and beryls, poison to destroy.
> Her rich robe of scarlet dye.

Six Criminal Women

   Her ribbons set with gold,   red gold, rare stones.
   Her array ravished me;   such riches saw I never.

The charges against Mede are of course wide and comprehensive, but one or two are accusations that had been brought against Alice Perrers in person.

   She taketh men's life and land   setteth law's prisoners free.
   She payeth the gaolers gold   to let the false go free and
                                                                    wide.
   With her jewels, by Jesus   she shameth your justices,
   She leadeth law where she pleases   and holdeth her courts.
   And maketh men through love of her   lose what justice
                                                                    oweth.

Another glimpse of the real figure we find in the line:

   For excommunication   she careth not a rush.

Langland was drawing a picture of the entire commonwealth, a vast satire on the whole structure of society. He merely borrowed the most outstanding piece of corruption of his time to body forth the spirit of corruption. He was not concerned with the later history of the woman whom he depicted in her fearful splendour. But the scarlet and golden idol was the same creature as the frustrated old woman, racked with covetousness and worn out with miserable longings. Her story has the symmetry and completeness which is seldom found in real life; it suggests some primitive legend of cause and effect.

THE LADY IVIE

The Lady Theodosia Ivie was born in 1623, and, in an age when many women of the upper classes could write little more than their own names and a recipe from someone else's cookery book, she became a crack forger. This in itself showed a degree of unusual if misdirected ability, and indeed, unpleasant as she was, Theodosia was one of the most striking women of her time.

Her father, John Stepkin, a medical man, was widowed when his daughter was a child. He was connected by marriage with a remarkable old lady called Mrs. Moundford, kind, capable, generous, who lavished her time and money on bringing up other people's children. Mrs. Moundford had been handsome, and even as an old woman she kept her straight, upright carriage. To the end of her life she could read without spectacles and walk without a stick. She had a wonderful knack of household management and of making people comfortable, and was "charitable to the uttermost, nay, beyond her estate and abilities". Her grandson, Sir John Bramston, who was a second cousin of Theodosia, says that when Mr. Stepkin asked Mrs. Moundford to take charge of her, Mrs. Moundford at first refused because her establishment was full. Mr. Stepkin, however, had no idea of being left with a motherless child on his hands, and would not take no for an answer. Theodosia was therefore brought up in the household in Milk Street. The comfort, decency, wholesomeness and good nature of Mrs. Moundford's regime were just what might be desired for a child's early years, but these good influences had singularly little effect on Theodosia.

Six Criminal Women

She was very beautiful, and though Mr. Stepkin did not produce a dowry for her, she made a reasonably good match with Sir George Garrett's son. She was married from Mrs. Moundford's house, and the marriage was said to have been happy while it lasted. Unfortunately the young man died a few years afterwards, and Theodosia, without a settlement and with no legacy but debts, was on her father's hands again.

John Stepkin did not intend this state of things to continue for longer than he could help. His daughter had nothing but her beauty, but that must have been considerable, for in an age when the dowry was a supremely important factor of the match it had already stood her in stead of money with one husband, and was to do so again. Her father now put on foot negotiations with young Mr. Anthony Browne of Weldhall in Essex. Stepkin and Theodosia were at this time living in Sir John Bramston's house, Skreenes, and here Stepkin brought young Mr. Browne to court her.

But Mr. Browne, either from habit or to keep his spirits up, had been drinking heavily, and when he bowed to Theodosia he was sick into her lap. Her anger and disgust were so great that she utterly refused to consider his proposal or even to see him again. Her father reasoned with her and abused her, but it was of no use. She was adamant.

It was not long, though, before the indefatigable Stepkin produced another suitor. This was Mr. Thomas Ivie, returned with a fortune from the East. He had had an honourable and distinguished career as an agent for the East India Company. His probable age is given by Sir John Fox as about forty-six at this time. Theodosia was twenty-six.

Ivie had come home full of eagerness to rejoin his wife, but she died as she was travelling to meet him. The bereavement, after some months of intense melancholy, left him very anxious to marry again.

The beautiful young Mrs. Garrett, well-connected though portionless, was represented to him as a desirable match.

The Lady Ivie

Mr. Ivie did not want money, his mind was set on marrying, and this lovely spirited girl, of whom, no doubt, the prudent father did not allow him to see too much, must have appeared to him not so much in her own image as in the shape of his desire.

For her part, Theodosia had had no opportunity to hear any harm of Mr. Ivie, since he had been out of the country for years. Then, too, he gave her magnificent presents. Among these were jewels worth many hundreds of pounds. Theodosia was acquisitive to a degree unusual even in the female sex, and his diamonds and rubies spoke for the suitor with a burning eloquence he himself did not possess.

More cogent than all, however, were the arguments of her father. Mr. Stepkin had landed an exceptionally fortunate catch, and he would not hear of Theodosia's refusing it. He told her bluntly that if she did not marry Mr. Ivie he would not keep her with him any longer. In other words, he threatened to put her into the street, and the idiom of the time made it quite possible that he would fulfil his threat. The woman of the seventeenth century who went against the wishes of her family while she was still unmarried was in a position of serious danger. Her strongest card in such a case was of course her parents' affection for her, but this card was not in Theodosia's hand. Her mother was dead, her father was John Stepkin. Had she been a child, her other relations would no doubt have stood between her and any outrageous treatment from her father. But she was a woman of twenty-six, and by this time, in the family circle at least, she must have been fairly well established as a vixen. If she were turned out of doors, there was no possibility of employment open to her except as a waiting gentlewoman to some more fortunate member of her sex, a form of bondage that would, one feels sure, have irked her to madness. Failing this, she must have thrown herself on the charity of one of her relations, or married the first man who offered to keep a roof over her head, and he might not have been as rich as Mr. Ivie.

The marriage took place in 1649. In the January of that year King Charles I had been beheaded, and this event had given a deadly shock to the nation as a whole, even to those who approved of the deed. The Cromwellian regime, though it had not finally crushed resistance, was at least firmly established. Loyalist adherents were heavily penalized and regarded with hostile suspicion, and the tempo of daily life was dominated by the stern supporters of a particularly unattractive brand of religious belief. We ourselves have read of the English Civil War and the French Revolution, and have lived to hear at first hand of the Russian Revolution. Nothing we might experience in a revolution could come with such a shock of unfamiliarity as the Grand Rebellion brought upon the ordinary inhabitants of England, when playhouses were shut, maypoles pulled down, estates confiscated, the pleasures of life were publicly denounced as sinful, and people loyal to the king were termed malignants.

The effect of these new conditions, the harsh restrictions, the cant terms, the ugly fanaticism of the ruling clique, must have made itself felt hourly to thousands, but ordinary life has an extraordinary way of going on, oblivious of governments. In the very years 1649 and 1650 Mr. Ivie gives a picture of the first eighteen months of his second marriage, passed as they were in London, the centre of the new administration, which reflects no influence from the political scene whatever.

The picture is in itself a remarkable one: it is not only the situation of the ordinary husband and the extraordinary wife which makes it so, or the throng of attendant characters whom they introduce, but it seems enhanced by the background against which it appears. In London, before the Great Fire, the Middle Ages remained not only in the looming pale Gothic landmarks of the Tower, the Abbey, West-

The Lady Ivie

minster Hall and London Bridge, but in a congested mass of small murky courts, of narrow cobbled streets, across which projecting upper storeys cast a shadow. The abominable slums into which no one but the indigenous dwellers ventured, the open sewers and unpaved lanes, the rotting heads stuck up on pikes over Temple Bar, were enclosed within the same small area as the fields full of may trees and cowslips beside Westminster, the gardens and orchards of Hatton Garden and Saffron Hill, and the beautiful domestic architecture of the Elizabethan, Jacobean and Caroline ages, houses of russet brick, striped with timber and dove-coloured stone, with diamond-paned windows and carved wooden portals.

The nobles' houses in the Strand with their massive stone water-gates adorned with dolphins and shells, the long-haired men in feathered hats and the women with hanging locks and wide rustling skirts, were part of the scene where men were hanged, drawn and quartered before gazing crowds, where the poor starved in the streets, and noise, rudeness, stench, and disease were separated by a few streets from an existence of exquisite cultivation and elegance, such as the late King had led in Whitehall. The whole city knew no stronger light than the sun and moon, whose absence was supplied by firelight, torchlight, candlelight; a deep glow, fitful gleams, a mild radiance that threw shadows deep as night.

Our own world is conditioned by a vast number of people living in a small space, requiring a ceaseless supply of goods made by machine and regimented by the routine of urban life, where a great proportion of our daily actions are automatic and only half-conscious; compared with this, the world of the seventeenth century, with all its discomforts and its horrors, was a world of intense feeling, of bold, imaginative expression. When people today sigh for the romantic past, they have probably very little idea of what they are asking for; half an hour spent watching an execution for high treason, a difficult childbirth at the hands of a seventeenth-century physician, or a walk through the town during a visitation of the plague, would no doubt have cured them of any such leanings; but in one sense their nostalgia is justifiable. They perceive, dimly, that in the pre-industrial ages not only was there, in everything man made, an aesthetic beauty, of which we now avidly preserve the few and scattered relics, but life was more "interesting" because it was lived on the plane of intense consciousness. The mechanical routine of factory, office, and suburban home leaves them hungry for this element, and they tend to search for it, vicariously, in gangster films and books, or in synthetic "period" romance.

In the medium of seventeenth-century existence the matrimonial adventures of Mr. Ivie take on an enlarged, exaggerated air. To us, they read like a story. There is no doubt, however, that they were real enough to him. They are found in his pamphlet: *Alimony Arraign'd*, published to announce his wrongs after the Lords Commissioners had granted his wife's application for alimony, and only two points suggest themselves in the consideration of the document as a true picture of the first eighteen months of this marriage: that some of the gross indecencies with which he charges his wife are admittedly hearsay, and that though her counter-charges are much less detailed and convincing, the Lords Commissioners, who saw both the parties, did in fact decide in the wife's favour. No doubt her great beauty did her case no harm, but one is inclined to believe that Mr. Ivie's pamphlet tells the truth rather than the whole truth.

Almost immediately after the wedding Mr. Ivie discovered, in his own words, that Theodosia had married his fortune rather than his person. None the less, he remained devoted and generous. Whatever the bride asked for was hers: coach and horses, a saddle horse whose trappings cost forty pounds, rich furniture, rich clothes, beds with the finest hangings

The Lady Ivie

and linen, and a never-ending supply of ready money. Mr. Ivie had given her in marriage settlements one thousand pounds a year, and the promise of one thousand in ready money at his death. In addition to the betrothal presents already made, he gave her twelve hundred pounds' worth of jewels. On the suggestion of John Stepkin, he gave his father-in-law a thousand down, in consideration of receiving, at Stepkin's death, the rents of an estate in Wapping, which amounted to two hundred and forty pounds a year. As Mr. Stepkin gave no sign of being near his end and was probably not much older than Mr. Ivie, his bargain was a good one.

Mr. Ivie had indeed been generous. He declared pathetically: "I laid down my fortune at her feet when I married her", and she availed herself of it so avidly that in his pamphlet he refrains from any detailed account of what he bought her and allowed her to buy; he said he did not want to be known for the fool he was.

But extravagance, however wild, could have been forgiven by a husband still under the spell of infatuation. What was intolerable was the crowd of spongers and disreputable hangers-on with whom his bride filled the house. There were, for instance, Sir William Killigrew and his son, both of whom were openly enamoured of her. There was young Mr. Snelling, whom any husband would have been tempted to kick downstairs. Worse than all, there was the bride's aunt, Mrs. Williams. This party had taken an immediate dislike to Mr. Ivie. She made use of offensive expressions about him, calling him a clown, a fool and an ugly fellow, and the very day after the wedding she had been caught making horns and mouths at him behind his back. Mrs. Ivie was given to fortune tellers. One whom she consulted (who had been cook-maid to Lady Gurney, but had now left service and set up as a clairvoyant) had foretold that Theodosia would live in peace with her husband for five years, whereupon Mrs. Williams "wished her hanged for her news". She openly aided and abetted Theodosia in every hostile act. Mr. Ivie ventured to ask his bride to keep some account of what she spent. Mrs. Williams thereupon told Theodosia that her husband's money was her money, and why should she keep account of her own? The habit of account-keeping for its own sake does not seem to have commended itself to this excellent woman.

Mr. Ivie made several attempts, not surprisingly, to forbid Mrs. Williams the house, but she was heard to say that she would keep his wife company in spite of his teeth. Mr. Ivie said in his pamphlet that neither she nor her husband had any private fortune, and no *ostensible* means of livelihood, yet they lived at the rate of several hundred pounds a year. How, he asked meaningly, was this managed? He supplied the answer in his description of Mrs. Williams's dwelling, a phrase that conjures up the obscure London of the 1650s—"a house of ill-fame, in a little blind alley".

Under Mrs. Williams's influence, or at least with her hearty encouragement, Theodosia showed a savage contempt for decency. Once she spent the whole day in Mr. Snelling's company at the Sugar Loaf in Long Acre, calling herself Mrs. Clarke; one night, she left her husband's bed, and on his asking her where she was going, she said, to her devotions, but actually she slipped downstairs and left the house with young Killigrew. Theodosia and her friends accused Ivie, among other acts of violence, of "squeezing her on the stairs". The truth of this incident was, he said, that once as she was preparing to leave the house near midnight on one of her nocturnal frolics he caught her by the arms to make her stay. Another night she leapt from his bed screaming out "Murder! Murder!" and a woman servant was brought in to say she had heard the screams; but, said Ivie, this woman had entered the house for the first time that evening, and her employment terminated the following day.

The Lady Ivie

She had merely been "planted" as a witness, a witness to nothing at all.

Poor Ivie said he had hoped that when he took a penniless wife, what was wanting in money on her side "would be made up in affection and sweetness to me". It was a natural expectation, but Mrs. Ivie's behaviour, though disagreeable and ungrateful to a degree, was not altogether unnatural either. She had been told flatly that if she did not marry Ivie her father would turn her out of doors. Was she to marry for his money a man nearly twice her age for whom she did not care a rap and then not to avail herself of his money? No, indeed. She was not one of those who submit to the kicks and neglect to pick up the halfpence. So far it is possible to feel a certain sympathy with her, but there were two incidents at least in Mr. Ivie's account of his domestic trials which show her in an ominous light. One was an attempt she made upon her brother (heard of on this occasion only) to murder her husband, by promising to keep his wife if he had to fly, and giving him a pass, procured from the Government, to carry him beyond the sea, which document Mr. Ivie then had among his own papers. The other was the extremely sinister story of Jenny Gilbert.

This was a young gentlewoman who waited on Mrs. Ivie as something between a companion and a personal maid. The girl was sickly but conscientious, and when Mrs. Ivie and Mrs. Williams suggested a party at Mr. Stepkin's one Saturday afternoon Jenny declined because she had a pile of lawn to starch and crimp before Sunday. However, the two women over-persuaded her. The visit was a trap. They took her instead to a quack doctor, who forcibly examined her and asserted her to be with child. Mrs. Ivie now declared that she had evidence to prove that her husband had betrayed her with Jenny Gilbert. The innocent girl defended herself fiercely. She was examined again by reputable doctors who confirmed that she was not pregnant. Still Mrs. Ivie persisted, and told the girl that if she would not confess to the intercourse Mrs. Ivie would say that she had made away with the infant by abortion. Jenny Gilbert showed an unexpected degree of passion in her resistance; and, fearing that the whole disgraceful business would come out, Mrs. Ivie found means to have her imprisoned as a spy in the service of the young exiled king. The case against her was palpably absurd, even to a suspicious revolutionary Government, and she was soon released, but she died very shortly afterwards.

That this scandalous piece of work could have gone on in Ivie's house without his getting to know of it till afterwards is one of the many extraordinary aspects of the story; thrown in among other accusations, the incident appears to have attracted little attention, but it gives some indication of the lengths to which Theodosia was prepared to go for an object on which she had set her heart.

The time came when economic pressure delivered Mr. Ivie from his intolerable existence. He was sick of keeping open house, at vast expense, for a pack of rascals, nor could he have continued to do so even had he wished it. His wife had embarrassed his affairs so much, that retrenchments were absolutely necessary. He told her they must retire to the country till their estate was recovered. Theodosia would not hear of any such thing. Had she married such a man as this to be buried with him in the country? Mrs. Williams, of course, supported her, so did her disreputable friends, fearing, as Mr. Ivie shrewdly said, "that if their Diana should leave London the silver shrine would also be removed".

However, he went on with his plans. He left London and went down to Wiltshire, where, at Malmesbury, was an old family house known as Malmesbury Abbey. This he bought from the present occupier, and when his establishment was ready, he wrote a most affectionate and conciliatory letter to Theodosia, asking her to make her

The Lady Ivie

arrangements for the move as soon as possible and to let him know when he should come to London to bring her down to Malmesbury. He explained in the letter that she had spent so much money recently that he could not immediately discharge her debts, therefore he gave her permission to sell the jewels for the purpose.

To this letter he had no reply. After some interval of complete silence, he had a communication, but not from Theodosia. It was a statement from the Lords Commissioners that his wife was suing him for alimony, on the grounds of cruelty and desertion.

In the seventeenth century a divorce could be obtained only by Act of Parliament. We have progressed since then, but in the matter of charging with cruelty and desertion a husband who simply wanted her to live in the country, Hollywood itself would have had nothing to teach Mrs. Ivie.

Her appeal to the Lords Commissioners said that her husband had left her destitute of the means of livelihood. "To which," said Mr. Ivie, "having sought patience from Above, I returned this answer . . ."

In the first eight months of the marriage she had spent eight hundred pounds on clothes, and in household expenses, two thousand eight hundred and seventy pounds.

If these sums are multiplied by twenty to give a conservative estimate of their value in modern money, it appears that she had spent more than seventy thousand pounds. No wonder that with these ferocious attacks on his fortune Mr. Ivie found himself unable to pay the promised jointure, though, as he had left jewels in his wife's hands, a part of which were worth one thousand two hundred pounds (or as we should reckon, twenty-four thousand pounds), and had told her to sell them, he could not be said to have left her destitute.

The petition which Theodosia laid before the Lords' Commissioners contained a list of grievances to match Mr. Ivie's own. She said he had dragged her about the room, "spraining her Joyntes", that he had brought on a miscarriage by knocking her down, and that she was so much afraid of him she had been obliged to hire a guard of soldiers. The accusations, horrible if true, do not carry so much conviction as the smaller grievances of Mr. Ivie, as of Mrs. Williams making horns behind his back the day after the wedding. Theodosia further accused him of having infected her with a disgusting disease, in answer to which Mr. Ivie produced a certificate signed by three eminent physicians, to say that he not only had not got the disease in question but so far as they could see he never had had it. Both Ivie and his wife went on to mutual accusations of such indecency that it is almost incredible to the modern reader that if they believed what they said they should ever have consented to live with each other again; yet Ivie's plea was that he should not have to pay the alimony but should have his wife restored to his arms; and in the ultimate reconciliation—or at least reunion—it was apparently Theodosia who made the first advance.

In her petition she was asking for alimony of three hundred pounds a year. The Lords Commissioners received Mr. Ivie's own statement of the case, but they decided in the wife's favour. Even allowing for the probability that some things came out of which Mr. Ivie in telling his own story makes no mention, the decision is still a wholesome reminder to us of how sweeping we are apt to be in our judgment of social conditions of the past. Women in the seventeenth century, it is often said, were the mere chattels of men; public feeling was always on the side of the man's rights against the woman's. One can only submit that Mr. Ivie did not find it so. He petitioned again and again that he should not be liable for this payment and that his wife should be told to return to him; and he asked the Lords Commissioners to choose some godly minister to live as chap-

The Lady Ivie

lain in the house, as a kind of make-peace between them. The Lords Commissioners, Puritans though they were, were men of the world. To Mr. Ivie's indignation, they "slighted" this proposal. As for Theodosia, she laughed aloud at it, "even in the presence of their lordships".

Mr. Ivie's determination not to be mulcted in this, as he considered, utterly unreasonable way gave rise to twelve separate actions, all arising out of the suit for alimony.

In 1660, the year of the Restoration, the couple were reconciled. Theodosia was now thirty-seven. Perhaps she now wanted a stable existence. She may have hankered after being a great lady in the country, and living admired and respected by her neighbours. Ivie seems to have done what he could to conciliate her. He admitted that the accusations in his pamphlet were shameful slanders, though one can more readily believe that he denied what he knew to be true for the sake of peace, than that such a man, of whom not much worse could be said than that he was a fool, should have published all those things when he knew them to be false. The couple lived at Malmesbury in outward tranquillity, and a daughter was born, called Frances.

In 1661 Ivie was knighted by the restored king, and Theodosia so much relished the title of Lady Ivie that she continued to call herself by it even when a third marriage had made her plain Mrs. Bryan. Even so, a certain amount of legal biting and scratching went on, though not perhaps more than experience should have taught Sir Thomas to expect. When he had married her, he had been pretty thoroughly taken in; but Providence, in the shape of the Lords Commissioners, had arranged to relieve him of his wife's society for the reasonable sum of three hundred pounds a year. As he himself had insisted on her return, he had only himself to thank for what happened after that. In the year of her child's birth he settled Malmesbury Abbey on Theodosia, and, according to her, he entered into a bond for ten thousand pounds to behave well by her and maintain her. In 1669 Sir Thomas wanted to come back to London, to retrench, as he said, Theodosia's notions of living in the country being almost as expensive as her ideas of town life had been. The result might have been predicted; as she had once refused to leave London, so she now refused to leave Wiltshire. Instead, she filed a bill in Chancery against her husband for the execution of the bond and brought an action against him in the Ecclesiastical Courts for cruelty and desertion. The result of these actions is not known. Three years later Sir Thomas died at Malmesbury, and so ended the first half of Theodosia's story.

She had the remains of Sir Thomas Ivie's fortune, and she had also the estate made over to her late husband by her father, John Stepkin. This estate consisted of land in Wapping, which, originally a marsh, had been drained by Van der Delf, a Dutch engineer, in the reign of Henry VIII. The greater part of it had been divided into two leaseholds, one of which was owned by the Dean and Chapter of St. Paul's, the other by an ancestor of the Stepkins who had bought it from the engineer. The value of both estates had during the past one hundred and twenty years enormously increased. The drained land had been cultivated and it was also being rapidly built up. The expanding population of London was increasing here, especially as several industries connected with shipping were being developed in the neighbourhood. The boundaries defined in the original leases were now difficult to trace out, as some landmarks (for instance a mill) could not be clearly identified with any such existing landmarks.

In 1673, the year before Sir Thomas's death, Theodosia began a series of actions against two small leaseholders, Whichcott and Bateman, claiming that their holdings were in fact a part of her own. The actions continued through 1673, 1675, 1676 and 1678. In some of these she was success-

The Lady Ivie

ful, in others the defendants maintained their claims. The key document in all these actions was a deed which became famous in Westminster Hall, and was called Glover's Lease; this deed was put in by Lady Ivie to prove that "one Richard Glover" was "in possession of certain lands by virtue of a long lease from Stepkins (sic) the Lady Ivie's ancestor".

In 1683 she began the action which became famous. In this, as H. B. Irving says, "True to the encroaching propensities of the plant that bears her name," she turned her attention to the other great leaseholder besides herself. This was a speculative builder called Thomas Neale, who held the lease given by the Dean and Chapter of St. Paul's. Lady Ivie declared that seven and a half acres of land in Shadwell, held by Mr. Neale, were a part of her own estate. The disputed terrain included a watermill, tenements, cottages, mansion houses, orchards, gardens, ponds, closes and the Manor of Stepney. Mr. Neale, who was a "projector" or speculator in town planning, had invested a good deal of money in the development of the area and he stood to suffer severely if the Lady Ivie made good her claim. This, however, she did. The court awarded her the property, their verdict being based to a large extent on two deeds of Mary Tudor's reign, known as Carter's Lease and Roper's Lease.

In the following year, however, the matter was reopened, on the ground that the verdict of 1683 had been secured by means of deeds that were forgeries.

The course of the second trial, in its labyrinthine windings and involvements, brings incidentally to light various startling passages in Theodosia's history, of which no detailed information had been available since Sir Thomas Ivie concluded his *Alimony Arraign'd*. She had married a third husband, a Mr. Bryan, who died early in 1684, and though she was now the widow Bryan, she preferred to call herself still the Lady Ivie.

The evidence of the trial reveals that during one of her

many quarrels with her husband Theodosia was taken in by Sir William and Lady Salkeld, who had a town house in St. Martin's Lane. They gave her hospitality and they lent her money, and Theodosia repaid their kindness, first by seducing their daughter's husband, an agile and unscrupulous gentleman called Mr. Duffett, and after Sir William's death by planning a large-scale robbery on the estate of his widow.

Mr. Duffett, like others before him, was bewitched by Theodosia, though at the time of their intimacy she must have been rising forty, an age at which, in that era, most women's romantic adventures were over. Mrs. Duffett was bitterly jealous of Lady Ivie, but, whether to spite her husband or not, she herself entered into an intrigue with a Mr. Frogmorton, and she behaved with such indiscretion that when she came to give evidence against Lady Ivie of an extremely damaging kind, her evidence was set aside on the ground that she was a disreputable woman whose word could carry no weight.

After Sir William Salkeld's death, Lady Ivie asked, in a feminine and unbusinesslike manner, how much she owed his estate. She was told ninety-six pounds. "Then, madam," she said to Lady Salkeld, "I will take four pounds to make it one hundred pounds." Notwithstanding this admission that she owed the estate one hundred pounds, she shortly afterwards produced a mortgage for one thousand five hundred pounds, which she said she had granted Sir William Salkeld on the house in St. Martin's Lane. This mortgage, according to Mrs. Duffett, had been forged by her husband, Lady Ivie and the latter's attorney, Mr. Sutton. The attorney said he could not draw the mortgage convincingly unless he had a sight of the title deeds. Lady Ivie obtained this for him by a piece of overbearing impertinence that shows the extraordinary strength of her personality. A part of the house was tenanted by Sir Charles Cotterell, and Lady Ivie

The Lady Ivie

discovered that Sir Charles had lent Lady Salkeld eighty pounds. She therefore urged Lady Salkeld, as a means of repaying this insignificant debt, to give Sir Charles a mortgage on the house of one hundred pounds. Sir Charles did not want any mortgage. He said that he was quite easy about the debt and that in any case as he was living in Lady Salkeld's house he could recoup himself if he wanted to by not paying rent; but Lady Ivie, with amazing interference, insisted that the arrangement she had proposed should be carried out. Mr. Sutton was employed to draw the mortgage for Sir Charles Cotterell. As he had therefore access to the title deeds, he was able to concoct the false mortgage for one thousand five hundred pounds. In the end the conspirators were not able to get the money; on Sir Charles Cotterell's becoming suspicious of its authenticity, Lady Ivie abandoned the mortgage. She had in the meantime borrowed from Sir Charles one thousand two hundred and fifty pounds, and out of this she paid Mr. Duffett two hundred pounds and Mr. Sutton another two hundred pounds.

This was a relatively early attempt of Lady Ivie's; she went on to far higher flights.

The verdict of 1683 had been, as before mentioned, based on Carter's and Roper's Leases, dated November and December 1555. These leases proved that the seven and a half acres of Shadwell, under dispute, were not part of the property of the Dean and Chapter of St. Paul's, from whom Neale was supposed to hold them, but were part of the estate of Lady Ivie's ancestor. The most important part of the immensely complicated trial of 1684 was the proving of these two leases to be forgeries. The proof was a small and simple matter, but of conclusive importance. It was merely a date. The documents were dated respectively November and December 1555, in the sixth year of Philip and Mary, whose titles were set out as follows: "By the Grace of God, King and Queen of England, Spain, France, both Sicilies, Jerusalem and Ireland, Defenders of the Faith, Archdukes of Austria, Dukes of Burgundy, Milan and Brabant, Counties of Hapsburg-Flanders and Tyroll."

But as pointed out by the prosecution, Philip's father, the Emperor Charles V, did not resign the crown of Spain until January 1556. Consequently Philip and Mary did not number Spain among their titles in 1555, and at that time were Princes only of the Sicilies and not king and queen. (It was a minor point that Milan should have stood before Burgundy.) This slip, a matter of only two months, but completely fatal once it had been detected, brought down the whole masterly edifice of the forger.

The trial opened in Westminster Hall on June 4, 1684, and the Lady Ivie was already so famous as a litigant that crowds had assembled in the spectators' benches and were jostled from the doors. The proceedings were heard by three judges. Except for a single remark by one of them, two remained mute throughout. This was not surprising, since the third was the Lord Chief Justice, Baron Jeffries.

The horrible reputation Jeffries earned by the last part of his career has completely obscured for the general reader any picture of him apart from the Bloody Assize. Nor is public opinion unjust. The atrocities of past centuries, when viewed in historical perspective, are sometimes seen to be understandable, if not excusable, but the barbarity stands utterly condemned which is condemned by the opinion of its own time. The first trial of the Bloody Assize, that of Alice Lisle, an old woman of eighty, who was accused of sheltering two fugitives from Monmouth's rebellion, was not printed until after Jeffries's death. As it was issued without his imprimatur, it is sometimes held that some of the worst things in it were written in afterwards to blacken James II's Lord Chancellor in the interests of the new regime of William III. But whatever might have been written in could scarcely blacken Jeffries worse than the

The Lady Ivie

sentence he actually pronounced. He sentenced Alice Lisle to be burned alive, and the utmost efforts of the Dean and Chapter of Winchester Cathedral only succeeded in altering the sentence to one of beheading. The horror this inspired was such that had the Bloody Assize ended there Jeffries's reputation would never have recovered.

The dark and lurid colours of his actions when he entered the political scene have overlaid the brilliant qualities of his professional career. Though Jeffries had not the mind of a great lawyer, in the practical attributes of a legal man he has perhaps never been surpassed. He had the grasp, the quickness, the penetration, the ready expression, all the ordinary qualities of a successful barrister, but he had them in a degree that was quite extraordinary. More than this, in the imaginative vigour of his speech, his vivacity and strong emotional response to the subject before him, he was, as Irving has said, almost like a character of Shakespeare's. As Dr. M. R. James says in the preface to Sir John Fox's edition of the Lady Ivie's trial, to read one of Jeffries's trials where no life was at stake and where he himself had no political bias, is a pure pleasure. His vitality, his shrewdness and humour, his racy, succinct turns of speech, are a perpetual stimulus and delight. Most people can be interesting when there is something interesting to say, but Jeffries informs the simplest comment with an animation all his own. It is literally true to say that with him on the bench there was never a dull moment. One has the full benefit of these gifts owing to the practice of the time which allowed the judge, if he wished, to conduct the cross-examining himself. Jeffries had an imposing array of counsel before him (the Lady Ivie's included the Attorney General, the Solicitor General and Sir Edward Herbert, who succeeded Jeffries as Lord Chief Justice), but he swept them aside continually, told them they did not know their business, questioned witnesses himself, lopping off irrelevancies and repetitions,

Six Criminal Women

explaining and clarifying the action at every point with his brusque, impatient efficiency.

The trial was one of the utmost complication and involved several issues. The first part of it was taken up with attempting to establish the boundaries of Neale's lease and that of Lady Ivie—whether the latter's territory were bounded by Fox's Lane or whether it extended to seven and a half acres beyond it. The central point in the prosecution's case was that two deeds on which Lady Ivie's claim depended had been forged, but no evidence was brought as to who had done these particular forgeries. In order, however, to support their point, the prosecution brought a large amount of evidence to show that Lady Ivie had forged other documents. Thus there were introduced, among other cases, the story of the forging of Sir William Salkeld's mortgage, and of the now famous Glover's Lease.

There was at least one thing to be said for Lady Ivie: there was nothing furtive about her. When engaged in the capital offence of forgery, she seems to have neglected even rudimentary discretion. The casual way in which the forgers were overlooked made the evidence so startling that even Jeffries was taken aback. Mrs. Duffet said:

"My lord, I did see Mr. Duffett forge and counterfeit several deeds for my Lady Ivie."

The Lord Chief Justice: "Do you hear what she says, Mr. Attorney General?"

The Attorney General: "Yes, my lord. We shall give an account[1] of her anon."

The Lord Chief Justice: "Truly, I hope I mistook her, and did not hear right what she said. Pray, mistress, speak it over again, and consider well what you say."

Mrs. Duffett: "I say, my lord, I did see Mr. Duffett forge and counterfeit several deeds for my Lady Ivie."

---

[1] The "account" given by Lady Ivie's counsel was of Mrs. Duffett having been seen in bed with Mr. Frogmorton.

The Lady Ivie

The first forgery Mrs. Duffett could name was Glover's Lease, on which rested Lady Ivie's claim to the lands of Whichcott and Bateman. The injured wife had a fine opportunity.

"Mr. Duffett was writing upon a parchment. I asked him what he was writing. He answered me he was counterfeiting Glover's Lease by which my lady would get many hundreds of pounds and for which he should have five hundred pounds. I desired him to consider what he did, for before that time he had been accounted a very honest man."

In describing the forging of the Salkeld mortgage, Mrs. Duffett explained the details of the actual process.

The Lord Chief Justice: "Was my Lady Ivie bye when the writing was made as you say?"

Mrs. Duffett: "She was bye giving him orders how to make it and what ink he should use to make it look old, and they forced me to make the ink, and to fetch saffron to put in it, to make it look old." She then described their methods of "distressing" the parchments. "They used to rub them on windows that were very dusty and wear them in their pockets to crease them. At other times," she said, "it was used to lay them in a balcony or any open place, for the rain to come upon them and wet them, and then the next sunshine day they were exposed to the sun, or a fire made to dry them hastily that they might be shrivelled." It was indeed characteristic that whereas Duffett wrote the ordinary black letter of the documents, he did not trust himself with the sweep of the great initials. These were done by Theodosia's hand. As Jeffries said in his summing up: "My Lady Ivie was so extraordinary an artist at the managing of such an affair that the master workman Duffett was not so dextrous at it as she; for he could not write the first great letters of the names that were to be put to the forged deeds, but she did that herself."

Mrs. Duffett gave this evidence again in 1687, when, the exposure of Lady Ivie as a forger having been made, the heirs of Whichcott and the creditors of Bateman tried to get the verdict originally given against them, reversed, on the ground that Glover's Lease was a forgery. On this occasion the Lord Chief Justice was Sir Edward Herbert, and he, like Jeffries before him, seemed scarcely able to believe his ears. "She said that in the year '70 or '71, she, coming into the dining-room of her house, the Lady Ivie and Mr. Duffe (sic) were there, and Mr. Duffe was writing. She asked him what he was doing. He answered he was forging, for the Lady Ivie, Glover's Lease." "Say again!" said the Chief Justice. "Are you sure he said he was forging Glover's Lease? She therefore repeated the words and said she was sure he said he was forging Glover's Lease."

The surprise occasioned by the late Mr. Duffett's insouciant manner of saying what he was doing was of course owing to the fact that forgery was a capital offence. Mr. Duffett stood to be hanged if he were found out, yet, on another occasion, there he sat calmly at the table in Mrs. Lee's kitchen, writing with his yellow-tinted ink, and this time Mrs. Elizabeth Rycott saw him. She said: "I did not know what they were that were written, but he said they were forged, and with ink out of those bottles he said he could make new writings look like old ones very soon."

Who Mrs. Rycott was is not explained, but she brought with her a packet of letters Mr. Duffett had given her, which she said he had told her were from Lady Ivie. They were indeed signed "T.I.", and Sir Charles Cotterell being appealed to in court as someone who knew Lady Ivie's hand, said he thought the writing was hers. The letters were read aloud by the clerk of the court. Unfortunately the contents have not transpired, except that one of them spoke of the Salkeld mortgage, and promised Duffett five hundred pounds if all went well. Their tone, however, can be gathered

The Lady Ivie

from Jeffries's reference to them: "They were very great together, that is plain, they were very familiar."

Lady Ivie herself, though the most important person present after Jeffries himself, was not allowed by the practice of the time to speak in a civil trial of which she was one of the parties. But the law and even the Lord Chief Justice could not oblige her to sit through such an occasion in complete silence. She burst out twice, on some evidence given by Sir Charles Cotterell, and twice Jeffries called her to order.

Lady Ivie: "You must give an account for what you have said here——"

The Lord Chief Justice: "Nay, madam, pray do not be in a passion; he has sworn what he has said here."

Lady Ivie: "If he doth swear it, he is forsworn."

The Lord Chief Justice: "Nay, madam, you must be more moderate in the court."

The jury found for Mr. Neale, that the seven and a half acres in dispute belonged to his lease and not to Lady Ivie's, and at the end of the trial Jeffries directed that the two forged leases should be impounded and that Lady Ivie should be prosecuted for forgery.

This trial took place in 1686. Her accomplice, Mr. Duffett, who had fled beyond the sea, had died before 1684, and the evidence of Mrs. Duffett was rejected because she had been seen in bed with Mr. Frogmorton, and it was apparently felt that no reliance could be placed on such a person. Well might Mr. Neale have exclaimed that the devil looks after his own. Indeed had Jeffries been on the bench again, it seems more than probable that a conviction would have been secured; but Jeffries was now Lord Chancellor, and his successor as the Lord Chief Justice was Sir Edward Herbert. This time "the jury scarce left the bar, but they found for my lady". Clearly Sir Edward Herbert made no hand of the matter.

Six Criminal Women

Lady Ivie's career had shown an amazing degree of boldness and arrogance in wrongdoing, but she achieved her climax in the will she left behind her. The verdict of 1684 had awarded the seven and a half acres to Mr. Neale as plainly as words could do it, but in her will, proved in 1695, she left this identical property, "all those houses, lands and tenements situate and being in Shadwell, extending from Fox's Lane to Ratcliffe Town," to trustees, to secure payment of her debts and legacies. Such was a high-spirited woman's contempt for the fiddle-faddle of the law.

One wishes no harm to Lady Ivie, but quite the contrary. She deserved well of the female sex when she refused to marry the disgusting young sot who was sick into her lap, and though there is a grimness about some of her doings which removes her from the realm of comedy into a darker sphere, there is an element of stimulus, of gaiety even, in the record of her activities. Mr. Neale described her as "famous for beauty and wit, and in law, cunning above any". But though cunning, she was clearly one of those beings who are animated by a sense of intense personal justification. Most of us say of our misdeeds: "I know it was wrong, but I felt I had to do it." The high-flying criminals, whose ranks Lady Ivie adorns, say, in effect, I did it, and I had a perfect right to do it! Seen from the safe distance of three hundred years away she is almost a sympathetic character, but none the less one cannot help regretting that she was not tried for her forgery by Jeffries. True, if she had been, she might very well have been hanged or transported beyond the seas, and that would have been a pity, but the trial would have been one of the forensic events of the century. If any human being could have put Theodosia down, it would have been Baron Jeffries; if ever a prisoner at the bar had been found able to give the Lord Chief Justice his own back again and something with it, it would surely have been the soi-distant Lady Ivie.

FRANCES HOWARD, COUNTESS OF SOMERSET

The bishops' preface to the Authorized Version of the Bible strikes a brilliant image when it speaks of "the setting of that bright Occidental Star, Queen Elizabeth of most happy memory", and it speaks with great justness of the "thick and palpable clouds of darkness" which arose on this event. We feel that the bishops descend to hyperbole only when they say that the clouds were dispelled by the appearance of James I, "like the Sun in his strength".

Certain epochs seem to us to have a tone, a tint even, which arises from the character of their thought, their poetry, their dress, painting, architecture. It is difficult to dissociate the Jacobean era from an aspect of gloomy richness, morbid elaboration, intellectual greatness that was enigmatic, and passion whose loveliness has turned to horror. The spirit of the age is reflected with strange consistency in its arts; the clothes, stiff, complicated and bulky, were conceived in a sombre, livid range of colours: in black and dim gold, in grey and lacquer red, in white and deepest crimson; their gems were milky, translucent pearls, black onyx, red cornelian. The great houses of the early seventeenth century have dark panelling, windows heavily leaded and blotted with coloured glass, and the heavy effect of the moulded plaster ceilings on which squat figures holding clubs or garlands are encircled with cumbersome strap-work, is intensified by plaster pendants hanging downwards. These effects, it may be said, belong as much to the last years of Elizabeth as to the reign of James: the great men, for instance, whose careers impart its character to the period were all figures of

Six Criminal Women

the preceding era. It is true that one cannot separate the tints of the rainbow, say where violet ends and indigo begins. It is only by comparing the centres of each period that one can make the contrast between the high summer of the Elizabethan and the autumnal weirdness of the Jacobean age.

Shakespeare's own contribution to the topical interest of a Scots king and an epidemic of witch-hunting is the appalling drama of *Macbeth*. More characteristic still are the plays of Webster and Tourneur with their moral anarchy and the fearful morbidity they exploit. *The Revenger's Tragedy* opens with Vendice sitting at his table with a skull before him and talking to it:

> *Thou shell of death, my study's ornament,*
> *Once the bright face of my betrothèd lady—*

The seventeenth-century theatre was the vehicle of popular taste, as the newspaper is today. This was a popular play. Can there have been any consonance between *The Revenger's Tragedy* and the tempo of daily life as the audience knew it? The answer is to be found in such a story as Frances Howard's.

The Howards were a Catholic family of great importance, though their fortunes had been chequered. Thomas Howard, Earl of Suffolk, was a cousin of the famous Elizabethan Admiral, Howard of Effingham. He had married a woman of unusual ability and unscrupulousness. Today she would have made his fortune in big business and the black market. Then, she made it by selling the preferments of which her husband had the disposal as Lord Chamberlain, and by other forms of political corruption even more remunerative. The balance of power throughout the reign of Elizabeth had been concerned with Spain as its most important element. With the prospect of a new monarch the buying and selling became even brisker. Several men and women of the court were

Frances Howard, Countess of Somerset

in Spanish pay. Prominent upon the pay roll of the Spanish Ambassador was Lady Suffolk, with a pension of one thousand pounds a year. It was commonly said that the Suffolks' great house, Audley End, on the borders of Cambridgeshire and Essex, had been roofed with Spanish gold.

Lady Suffolk had been a beauty till she was spoiled by smallpox. The influence of beauty was now lost to her, and she lived only to amass money, build up the family consequence and manipulate the lives of her children.

She had three daughters, of whom the two eldest were married to the Earl of Banbury and Lord Cranborne, the son of Robert Cecil, the Secretary of State. Frances, like the youngest daughter in a fairy tale, was the most beautiful of the three. Her sisters were trollops, but she as a child was gentle, well-mannered and self-contained. If anything, in the light of later events, could make her seem more alarming this would be it.

The young Earl of Essex was kindly regarded by the new king. His father, Robert Devereux, had lost his head for his rebellion in Elizabeth's last years, but James had restored his father's estates to the boy, and it seemed that he might prosper as a royal protégé. The Suffolks, anxious to sweep any potential asset into their net, offered the fourteen-year-old earl the hand of their thirteen-year-old daughter.

The earl was a preternaturally grave boy, with heavy features and fine eyes. He formed the greatest possible contrast to the sprite-like creature who was still too young to have burst into the beauty that was afterwards famous. The wedding was held with great magnificence. The marriage masque was written by Ben Jonson and mounted by Inigo Jones. The courtiers were dressed so fine in jewels and feathers it was thought that the banqueting hall in which the masque was held must have contained every jewel and every rope of pearls to be found in the City of London. The splendours were bright but empty. The pair were too young to consummate the marriage, and they were separated after the revels. The earl went to France to finish his education, the countess went home to Audley End.

Here in the great house, remote, enclosing a world of its own, she had the unimproving society of her mother and the even more baneful influence of another relation.

Her father's uncle, Henry Howard, Earl of Northampton, was one of those people who stand as a picture of their times. He was intellectual, super-subtle, unmoral, vainglorious, rich. His elder brother, the Duke of Norfolk, had been beheaded by Elizabeth's government for supporting Mary Queen of Scots. Some kindness had been shown to the younger brother, but Howard had known many vicissitudes

—and expectations vain
Of Princes' courts which still do fly away.

He had been brought up in luxury and educated at Cambridge, and he had known what it was to go without a dinner and to have no means of reading except turning over the books exposed for sale in Paul's Churchyard. These memories no doubt fanned his almost maniacal lust for wealth and power. He now lived in fantastic splendour. He was a bachelor, a bon-viveur, a scholar, an intriguer, an architect. His mansion in the Strand was built to his own plans and he advised his nephew in the building of Audley End. When he came up to town from the country sixty retainers accompanied him. His passion for worldly goods was so engrossing that in his last illness he begged the king that none of his enemies might have the offices which his death would leave vacant.

As a man of the world, of great reputation and considerable charm and in the easy domestic circumstances of a bachelor, he naturally fascinated young people and he himself enjoyed their society. Several young persons had been

Frances Howard, Countess of Somerset

warned against his dangerous acquaintance. Old Lady Bacon wrote to her son Francis:

"Avoid his familiarity. . . . I have long known him and observed him. His workings are stark naught."

There was no one to warn his grandniece against him and in any case the warning would have been useless. Such an uncle was bound to have a powerful influence on such a child, if he chose to exert it. Her extreme youth, her beauty, her agile wits, her discretion, her devotion to himself, could not but charm him. To the childish countess the retirement of Audley End was the more tedious after that scintillating brief interlude in which she had played the leading part and whose glories had vanished as abruptly as a shooting star. The tediousness, however, was enlivened when her uncle Northampton came on a visit, and his visits were frequent.

Northampton, as a Howard and a Catholic, naturally adhered to the Spanish interest. He was a Catholic purely in what might be called the political sense, for his behaviour was totally irreligious and his loyalty to his fellow Catholics was non-existent. But he was heart and soul attached to the pro-Spanish policy. There his sincerity admitted of no doubt. In the family conversations at Audley End it would sound, to the ears of an attentive child, as if the most important thing in the world were that the power of the Howard family should be maintained, that the Spanish policy was a means of maintaining this supreme good and was therefore part of it, and that everybody who stood in the way of the Howards or opposed the Spanish alliance was bad and worthless, had in fact forfeited the rights of a human being and should be got rid of almost as a duty.

Northampton was in the closest touch with the court and nothing escaped him of "who's in, who's out, who loses and who wins", so that when another young person began to make himself remarkable Northampton kept an eye on him and never rested until he, too, was in the Howard net. Among the train of followers who had accompanied the king from Scotland, eyed askance by the English as "beggarly Scots", sharp-set to eat them up, was a young man called Robert Carr. He attracted the king's notice when a horse threw him at a tournament and he was picked up with a broken leg. He was rather tall, very well made, with wide-apart, somewhat blank and smiling eyes, flaxen hair on his head and a moustache and beard of ginger colour. He was a page, the son of a gentleman, but with next to no education, without cultivation, experience or brains; with no assets, in fact, but a certain native shrewdness, a good appearance and a cheerful disposition. The two last were, however, exactly the two qualities needed to please the king, and more solid ones would have spoilt the effect that James required. The king's fondness for young men, however perverse in its nature, was partly that of a nervous being who cannot endure the least criticism and who finds in young and inferior people the uncritical reverence and enthusiastic gratitude which soothe and inspire him. The situation created by this leaning is almost bound to end in disaster as it corrupts the good qualities of the younger person by giving him too much fine fortune and requires a standard from him to which he is quite unequal. The best that can be said of Carr is that he could have been worse than he was. He was a tolerably decent young man, not ruined quite so completely or quite so soon as might have been the case. His situation at best was not altogether enviable, as it depended on a close intimacy with the king whose character was an astonishing mixture of qualities that were baffling, painful and disgusting. James's intermittent shrewdness and acumen were so great that when they operated they placed him head and shoulders above the people who surrounded him. He had an idea of maintaining the world's peace. He was one of the few men of his time who could even approach Bacon on

Frances Howard, Countess of Somerset

terms of intellectual equality. This was the same man whose lack of judgment, obstinacy and incompetence paved the way for the Puritan revolution, while his emotional nature was no less complicated than his intellect; the indecorous old fool was capable of tender affection and occasionally stands revealed in the dignity of real anguish.

James's Secretary of State was Robert Cecil, who had inherited his position from his father during Elizabeth's last years. When Lord Burleigh advised the son who was to succeed him, he told him that he should never try to overpersuade the queen; her ability and experience were so great that if left to her own judgment she would form a shrewder opinion than anyone else. It was the minister's duty to watch until after long shudderings and quiverings the needle pointed true, and then to set the compass by it. This attitude to statecraft, one of co-operation between the highest specialists, is in staggering contrast to that of the succeeding reign, in which Robert Cecil found himself superseded in the king's intimate councils by a young man to whom the king was teaching Latin in the mornings. James, of course, meant the political relationship, like the emotional one, to be that of master and pupil. He intended to form Carr in his own image and so to imbue him with his own political wisdom that the pupil would be able to deputize faithfully for the master, to be his attuned instrument among many discordant notes. Meantime the brighter side of Carr's fortune was dazzling, in his own eyes and those of the needy young men who had recently been his companions. The grants, increasing in size and number which swelled his income, the encouragement he received from the king to dress richly, fashionably, with constant change, the exquisite jewels he was given, including the king's portrait set in diamonds, the presents he got from everyone who hoped to enjoy his patronage, the homage of elderly, distinguished men who had previously been in another sphere from his own, and who had been unaware of his very existence: all this not only gratified all his wishes for material things, but it gave him an almost magical status. The obscure young man was now treated as if he were a young god. Yet he had to pay somewhat dearly for all this. He had to tolerate the affectionate demonstrations of a man whose great qualities he could scarcely appreciate and whose grotesque attributes were but too patent to everybody. James "was of middle stature, more corpulent in his clothes than in his body, yet fat enough, his clothes being made large and easy, the doublet quilted for stiletto-proof, his breeches in great pleats and full stuffed . . . his eyes large, ever rolling after any stranger that came into presence . . . his tongue too large for his mouth, which ever made him speak full in the mouth, as if eating his drink which came out into the cup on each side of his mouth". He did not wash very much. His legs were so weak that he was always "leaning on other men's shoulders". He had a habit of hanging round the necks of those he was fond of, and slobbering their cheeks.

Not only had Carr to make himself agreeable in these unpleasing circumstances, but he had also to undergo a good deal of work for which he was quite unfitted. He might enjoy deputizing for the king in admonishing Prince Henry —that cold and haughty young man—about his marriage, or advising the king to dismiss Parliament when the Commons grew threatening in their behaviour. But when it became a matter of reading every despatch that came from an ambassador at Paris, the Hague, Rome, Madrid, Lisbon or Muscovy; of being expected to deal with all the tiresome minutiæ of arbitrary government: the coinage, licences, import duties, penal laws against Catholics, irregularities in the judicial system and the intransigence of the Irish—it was too much. Anyone in this position would have needed a secretary. Carr needed something more—a secretary, an adviser, a true friend, another self, to enable him to be and

Frances Howard, Countess of Somerset

do all the things that his glorious and heavy fate required of him.

He had made the acquaintance some years before of a young man called Thomas Overbury, and, drawn perhaps by the attraction of opposites, the two had become firm friends. Overbury, whose portrait by Isaac Oliver can be seen in the Bodleian, was a man of remarkable capacity. He was also of a difficult temperament. It was said of him that it was his failing to think too well of himself and too little of everybody else. Looking at Oliver's miniature with its pale forehead and dark eyes, its suggestion of a domineering and critical temper, its expression of resentment just tempered to a decent calmness, it is easy to understand this stricture. Carr was fair, and Overbury dark; Carr was open and debonair, Overbury was secret and black-avised; Carr was radiant with a magnetic physical attraction, Overbury had few friends and his passion was ill-starred.[1] Above all, Carr was not clever and Overbury was. The path of the two was inevitably marked out. Overbury could do for Carr exactly what Carr needed and what no one else could do so well.

He and Carr, two penniless young men without backing, had begun their career neck and neck, except that it seemed as if Overbury were the better equipped to succeed of the two. But nothing had gone right with him. Robert Cecil had promised to befriend him, but nothing had come of that. Overbury hung about the court and he made the acquaintance of Ben Jonson, who thought well of him, but they afterwards quarrelled. Overbury wrote the remarkable *Characters,* mostly of types whom he disliked: A Hypocrite, An Ignorant Glory-Hunter, A Canting Rogue, An Affected Traveller, a Very Whore. He travelled in the Low Countries and wrote a book about them: *Observations on the Seventeen Provinces.* Always it was his lot to be admired, but not

[1] He had wanted to be the lover of Lady Rutland.

successful. Carr's fate had been exactly the opposite. In the blink of an eye the impossible had happened to him, his transfiguration had occurred. He had been kind and generous to his friend. He had procured him a knighthood, some grants, but with all his efforts Overbury's fortunes had not taken root. In 1611 Overbury was back at court again, and Carr, now Viscount Rochester and more glorious than ever, needed his services.

The place meant money, but that was of relatively little importance to Overbury. It meant, above all, the excitement of power, of influence, which he had been denied so long and which he would otherwise never have had a shadow of opportunity to obtain. True, the position was not entirely satisfactory. Carr, the good-natured, the complacent, the dunderhead, was the master; Overbury the astute, the intellectual, the gifted, was either Carr's servant, or he was nothing—he could take his choice. He took it and he served faithfully.

At first it was enough for him to be allowed to get his hands on the work. What was an irksome task to Carr was of absorbing interest to Overbury. His method was to read everything himself and keep Carr primed in the essentials by word of mouth. Carr soon gave up reading documents altogether. The despatches came to him, he passed them unopened to Overbury, who undid the seals, made notes of the contents and passed them to the king. In Bacon's words: "I will undertake the time was when Overbury knew more of the secrets of state than the council did." It was true that Overbury was Carr's creature, but it was equally true that Carr was Overbury's, and anyone who had noticed the latter's strange face might have foretold that one day Carr would find himself, like the Arabian fisherman, overshadowed by a djinn who refused to go back into the bottle.

The young Countess of Essex was now fifteen, and Lady Suffolk, no doubt as willing to leave Audley End as her

Frances Howard, Countess of Somerset

daughter was, brought her to London. Frances's beauty made a sensation. The contemporary historians all appear to have disliked her, except David Lloyd, who describes her as "a lady of transcendent beauty and full of fire", but all, like him, are agreed upon her loveliness, that she was "a beauty of the first magnitude".

One of the many revels of the year 1610 was a superb masque, The Triumph of Tethys, in which the queen appeared as the mother of the rivers and the Princess Elizabeth as the river Thames. Twelve peeresses impersonated twelve other rivers and some attempt was made to fit each lady with a river already in some way associated with her. As one of the Earl of Essex's possessions was Bennington in Hertfordshire, "a very gallant seat", the young countess was to impersonate the "crystal-streaming Lea". The clothes, designed by Inigo Jones for the river nymphs, were poetry in themselves. Their sky-blue taffeta skirts were covered with waving lines of silver and silver marine creatures. Round their waists were massive draperies of cloth of silver, embroidered with gold sedge and seaweed. Their heads were crowned with shells and coral, and on the very top of each head a murex shell fastened a transparent floating veil. The queen spoilt the effect Jones had desired by insisting on a costume of her own, but the river nymphs numbered at least two exquisite beauties among them, those of Thames and Lea. Of these two, the latter was by far the more suited to such a display. Frances Howard had, besides her unusual beauty, the boldness, collectedness and the strong enjoyment of public admiration, which made her charms appear to the utmost advantage.

Her husband was still abroad, but he was in being and he was shortly expected home, therefore Frances's career as a court beauty could operate only within a limited sphere. A marriage was out of the question, and a liaison with her, unless conducted with the utmost discretion, might entail very serious consequences. Notwithstanding, she entered upon one of the most exalted kind. James's elder son, the Prince Henry, was a serious-minded, chaste young man, at variance with his father on almost every point. He supported his mother, the neglected Queen Ann of Denmark; he fiercely despised and abominated Carr; he enjoined sober habits on his household. Drunkenness was forbidden and everyone who swore had to put a contribution in the poor's box. He was anti-Catholic and anti-Spanish, and he had a deep friendship with Sir Walter Raleigh, who was enduring an eighteen years' imprisonment in the Tower as a sacrifice to the king's Spanish policy. Raleigh had told the boy about his adventures, talked to him about the History of the World, and written for him directions as to how a man of war should be built for speed in sailing. "No one but my father," said the prince, "would keep such a bird in a cage." The prince had never had a mistress, but he became passionately enamoured of the very slender girl with a pale face, dark grey eyes and light, crinkled hair, which when it was undone came to her knees. Lord Essex was in France, and no Prince of Wales could ask for a chaperone more indulgent than Lady Suffolk. It was the general opinion, though still denied by a few of his admirers, that the prince had taken a mistress at last.

Ambition would have carried his cause with Frances had he been less agreeable than he was; but not for long. Though charming, he was not a man to make a deep impression on her; he was grave and idealistic, and in any case he could not make her a queen. Had she been free herself, he was destined for an Infanta or a French princess. Her enigmatic grey eyes, that looked so dangerous to men of the world, had already lighted on another object. Prince Henry doted on her till he realized that she was favouring another admirer and that his rival was the detested Carr. At a ball, Lady Essex dropped one of her gloves, and an officious courtier,

Frances Howard, Countess of Somerset

thinking to gratify the Prince of Wales, picked it up and brought it to him. There was a pause as the onlookers waited for the interesting moment. "I will none of it," said the Prince loudly. "It hath been stretched by another."

Frances did not receive humiliation lightly; she was vindictive to a degree, but she was not able to punish the Prince of Wales. If he chose to remove himself from the sphere of her attraction she could not harm him. In any case the humiliation of this moment was somewhat lessened by her intense preoccupation with another man. Whatever the prince or anyone else might say or do, so long as it did not interfere with the success of her passion, belonged to that realm of consciousness which is separated from the vital centre of the being and is seen like something happening outside a window. Once she was under the spell of sexual passion she showed that removedness of mind which is next door to moral imbecility. That she was extremely cautious in her conduct may be supposed partly from the manners of the time and partly from the fact that with attraction on Carr's side and so much passion on hers there was need or even opportunity for a prolonged courtship. The stately ritual of love-letters, compliments, tokens, by which love was declared in high life, was carried on between the stiffly-clothed figures like the movements of a pavanne. Letters full of tortuous simile and elaborate sentiment were a necessary part of the proceedings, and Overbury wrote Carr's with effortless skill. This part of his secretarial duties cost him scarcely a thought. He disliked Frances Devereux, but he did not regard the matter as anything of importance. Provided Carr could keep out of any serious trouble when the husband should return, Overbury thought that a liaison with the most celebrated young beauty of her time was to Carr's credit rather than otherwise. The probability would appear to be that the pair had become lovers very shortly before Essex arrived home to claim his bride in 1611.

Six Criminal Women

The girl's situation was now frightful. Devoured by passion for a lover, filled with resentment and loathing by a heavy, solemn young husband, she saw herself dragged away to the earl's seat in Staffordshire while Carr remained in London. All the women at court would be trying for him, and while she was buried in the country he would forget her. She was but seventeen and nearly frantic.

She was quite untouched by religion; even in an age when it was in some sort a living reality to almost everyone it meant nothing to her. Her maid said that the countess never came to prayers. But she had a strong belief in another form of the unseen: in magic, clairvoyance and witchcraft. She had found out a Mrs. Ann Turner who lived at Hammersmith, and was the widow of a doctor, a gentlewoman who had come down in the world. Mrs. Turner had many avocations; one of them was fashionable millinery. She had brought out of France a system of stiffening ruffs and cuffs with yellow starch. The French had found the yellow tint more becoming to their sallow complexions than pure white, but the English also had adopted the fashion with enthusiasm, and Mrs. Turner's yellow starch had made her name at court. She had also less reputable means of income. She was said to be a procuress, and it is certain that she was the business associate of a disreputable though extraordinarily interesting man, a friend of her late husband's. This was Dr. Simon Forman, who lived at Lambeth. He seems to have combined genuine learning and a power of natural healing with a little clairvoyance and a good deal of quackery. His own account of his doings (which unfortunately does not cover his dealings with Mrs. Turner) is of fascinating interest: his early misadventures, the curious hallucinations he experienced, his struggles to get himself an education, his success at last in a thriving practice. It is satisfactory to know, since he was ostensibly a doctor, that though he was "judicious and fortunate in horary questions,

Frances Howard, Countess of Somerset

especially theft, and had good success in resolving questions about marriage", yet "sickness was his masterpiece". Lady Essex was brought to the doctor by Mrs. Turner, and he undertook to do two things: to inflame Carr's passion for her and to render the Earl of Essex impotent. These feats were to be accomplished by drugs and potions and the making of little images in brass and wax to represent the parties. Lady Essex called him "Sweet Father" and paid him liberally. He assured her that if she placed the matter in his hands she need not fear even if her husband did carry her away into the country. Mrs. Turner increased her confidence in Dr. Forman by telling her of what the doctor had done for Mrs. Turner's lover, Sir Arthur Manwairing. His spells had caused this gentleman to ride furiously through a violent storm during the night hours till he arrived at Mrs. Turner's house without knowing what had brought him there.

Frances was a little consoled by these professional consultations, but her situation still seemed desperate to her. Now that the earl had returned, Carr had, naturally enough, withdrawn his attentions. This was distracting to her, and she had at the same time to fend off the advances of her eager husband. This at first she was able to do by pretending to be shy and frightened. The earl was only eighteen and he was particularly gentle and considerate in his treatment of women. He had fallen in love with the beautiful creature when he saw her again, but he was willing not to force his passion on her. At the same time her way of behaving herself in the society of the court was displeasing to him. Essex was a Puritan—(in later life he became a general in Cromwell's army), and as a young man of eighteen he disapproved of fashionable and worldly pursuits. He asked his wife to be "less often abroad and more civil at home", but he might as well have spoken to the wind. At last he appealed to his father-in-law. The Earl of Suffolk was practically a cipher in his family, but he put in his word for what it was worth and said that the time had now come when the couple should live together as man and wife. Fortified by this pronouncement, the Earl of Essex prepared to remove to Chartley, his house in Staffordshire.

A member of the earl's household who afterwards became his secretary was a young man called Arthur Wilson. He abhorred the countess because he loved his master, and when as an elderly man he wrote his *Memoirs of the Reign of James I,* though most of the actors were dead and the scenes he described had long passed away, the young husband's sufferings were still vivid in his mind and he described the woman who caused them with vitriolic hatred. Though Wilson's animosity underlines every word, he was a recorder of exceptional skill. He was extremely sensitive to the values of any scene (it was he who gave the exquisite picture of the wedding of the Princess Elizabeth to the Elector of Bohemia, in which the bridal retinue of girls in white gemmed with diamonds looked like the Milky Way). Much as he hated the countess, he never withheld tribute to her beauty, "her indeed lovely cheeks", and his perception of emotion in other people makes his account extraordinarily lively. "How harsh was the parting," he exclaims, "being rent away from the place where she grew and flourished! Yet she left all her engines and imps behind her; the old doctor and his confederate Mrs. Turner must be her two supporters; she blazons all her miseries to them as they depart and moistens the way with her tears. Chartley was an hundred miles from her happiness, and a little time thus lost is her eternity."

Unaccommodating as his wife had been in London, it was not until they got down to Chartley that Essex found out what she was really like. It was the height of summer, but the countess ordered all the windows of her apartments to be darkened and would not leave her rooms except for an

Frances Howard, Countess of Somerset

hour or two when the household was asleep. The earl, who was obliged to visit her by candle-light, found her utterly intractable. Long periods of sullen silence were succeeded by storms of violent abuse. He shared her bed, but she refused to yield herself to his embraces, and Wilson says that Mrs. Turner had provided her with a device that would make a consummation of the marriage impossible.

Had the earl been older, more experienced, of a more ruthless disposition, he might still have been no match for the creature beside him. The methods she was afterwards discovered to have employed were no doubt useless in themselves, but they could only have been used by a woman of utter criminality. Debilitating powders were given to the earl and by winning over his personal servants to herself she ensured that his body linen and the sheets of his bed were all steeped in some infusion which Dr. Forman has assured her would "imbecillate" the earl and make him impotent. But though she believed in the power of these methods, she was terrified that they might not be found sufficient. She wrote desperately to Mrs. Turner.

"Burn this letter.

"Sweet Turner, I am out of all hope of any good in this world for my father and my mother and my brother said I should lie with him and my brother Howard was here and said he would not from this place all winter so that all comfort is gone, and which is worst of all my lord hath complained that he hath not lain with me and I would not suffer him to use me. My father and mother are angry but I had rather die a thousand times over for besides the sufferings I shall lose his [Carr's] love; if I lie with him I will never desire to see his [Carr's] face if my lord do that with me." "As you have taken pains for me all this while," she said, "so now do all you can—for never so unhappy as now; for I am not able to endure these miseries that are coming on me, but I cannot be happy as long as this man liveth . . . if I can get this done you shall have as much money as you can demand, this is fair play. Your sister, Frances Essex."

Her letter arouses compassion; it also shows the writer's temperament with startling distinctness. To such a mind there is no alternative to accomplishing its desire.

For nearly two years this extraordinary warfare was maintained. The countess consented to give up her seclusion and her darkened rooms. She stayed with her husband at various great houses, where they appeared to be on decently civil terms with each other, a deception favoured by the elaborate ceremonial of the day. The waiting women declared that the earl and countess slept naked in the same bed. But one morning the countess mislaid a ruby pendant which she wore attached to an ear-ring and she asked her gentlewoman to see if it had been dropped in the bed. The lady and one of the chambermaids pulled off the bedclothes and they saw the two indentations in which the husband and wife had slept, so far apart that they could not have touched each other.

Arthur Wilson, with a clear-sightedness remarkable in an age when belief in witchcraft was widely held, discusses the effect of suggestion which was credited to magic. "Her courtly invitements that drew the viscount to her she imputed to the operation of those drugs he had tasted, and that hardness and stubborn comportment she expressed to her husband making him (weary of such entertainment) to absent himself, she thought proceeded from the effect of those potions and powders that were administered to him. So apt is the imagination to take impression of those things we are willing to believe." "We could dispute the nature of these operations," he says, "how far they are contingent and how far the faculty works with them though ignorant of them . . . for we will never allow there was any other diabolical means used, nature being strong enough for such a production."

Frances Howard, Countess of Somerset

In the November of 1612 the whole country was filled with horror by the sudden death of Prince Henry at eighteen years of age. It is supposed now that he died of typhoid fever. The general belief at the time was that he had been poisoned. Suspicion rested on many people. The king himself, some thought, had made away with the elder son, who was hostile to him, to put his favourite Prince Charles in his place. Others thought that the Prince of Wales had been murdered as part of a far-reaching Catholic conspiracy which had begun with the Gunpowder Plot and aimed at destroying the whole royal family. Others again suspected the favourite Carr, since the enmity between the two young men was notorious; and this belief, for which no evidence has ever been produced, was strangely persistent. King Charles I told one of his friends that he had always believed that Carr murdered his brother. Beneath the storm of agitation, fear and grief which filled the air, the topic of poisoning sounded its sinister, recurrent note. Three months later, in February 1613, a curious prosecution was opened at Norwich and then allowed to drop. A "wise woman" of the neighbourhood, known as "Cunning Mary", who told fortunes and sold charms, was accused by a pursuivant on behalf of Lady Essex of stealing a diamond ring and a gold cup. The woman said that Lady Essex had given her these things in return for an undertaking to poison the Earl of Essex by means of a slow poison which should work at a distance of three or four days. Cunning Mary, however, had repented of this wicked design and had left London. The countess's indignation at being bilked of her gold and diamonds had outrun her discretion, but some powerful means, unnamed, were used to repair this blunder, for after a second examination the woman was let go and no more was heard of this awkward matter.

The earl and countess were now living for part at least of the time at court, and the liaison between the countess and Carr was resumed, with intense delight but with equal secrecy. Mrs. Turner arranged meetings for the lovers at her house at Hounslow, and sometimes, when this proved too distant for the brief time Carr could spend out of the king's sight, at a lodging in Paternoster Row. Carr was now, after the king, the most powerful man in the kingdom. He was Lord High Treasurer of Scotland, Knight of the Garter, Privy Councillor, and on Cecil's death in 1612 the king had made him First Secretary. The Earl of Northampton regarded his young friend with an anxious and an avid eye. Carr's position was so powerful that it threatened the supremacy of the Howards. If the Howard family were to maintain their grip on the main source of the kingdom's wealth a close alliance with Carr was now of the first importance to them.

The pieces stood before Northampton on the board; nothing was wanting but the direction of the skilful player. It cannot be said who started the idea, but it took shape from Frances's childish habit of confiding in her great uncle. Northampton did not take long to realize that the marriage which was no marriage, with a young woman who had turned out not to be worth the Howards' alliance, could by a stroke of exceptional boldness be changed for a marriage with a young man whose alliance meant everything to the family fortunes. There was only one way of doing this, but after the lamentable history of the Essex marriage it was the obvious way. It was decided that the Countess of Essex should sue for a divorce on the grounds of nullity.

The Earl of Essex at first refused to be party to such a proceeding, but then the pangs of his despised love and the misery of his domestic life decided him to undergo this final humiliation so that it might be the last. Willing, as Wilson says, "to be rid of so horrid a mischief", he agreed with Northampton and Suffolk that he would not oppose the suit.

The king was not jealous of his favourite's love of women,

Frances Howard, Countess of Somerset

and he was ready to forward the match with Frances Howard as a means of pleasing Carr. But one among Carr's party opposed it with violent bitterness. In Overbury's subtle mind there were no doubt objections of many kinds, but some were definite enough. He strongly disapproved of the Howards, for he was anti-Catholic and anti-Spanish in his political views. He knew that despite the servility, the adoration even, which Carr commanded by his position, he was in reality exceedingly unpopular. The queen hated him for being her husband's favourite; the court were jealous of him, and some actually called him murderer; the country hated him as the type of the proud, beggarly Scot who injured them by his greed and insulted them by his arrogance. In Overbury's view, Carr ought not to risk a tumble, and what a risk he ran here! He was Carr's second self, and he knew all about the liaison with Lady Essex, for he had helped it on himself. He knew something even more damaging. In her passionate anxiety to retain her lover Lady Essex had told him all she had done to keep herself for him alone. If this, or even a part of it, should come out, the scandal would be such that even Carr's great eminence would be threatened. Besides all this, Overbury, like Arthur Wilson, detested the young countess. Whether he were jealous of his friend's passion for her, or whether his haughty nature resented some slight she had put on him, at all events he opposed the marriage, not only with sound argument, but with a deep personal bitterness. He told Carr that the woman for whom he proposed to risk his career was nothing but a whore. This, in our use of the word at least, was not true; no one was ever less accommodating than Frances Howard. He also said the marriage would ruin Carr. There he was entirely right.

The situation developed into an open quarrel of the harshest kind. Overbury had now for some time been feeling his feet. He knew that as regards the actual work of the administration it was he and not Carr who was the important man. It was said: "The king trusted Carr with his despatches and Carr trusts Overbury a month together without examination, who had full commission to receive and answer any letters or other expresses that came to his hands.". Yet in himself he knew that he was nothing. It was Carr who possessed the magic. The situation had always been humiliating, but once he had accepted it willingly for the sake of its advantages. Now that he knew the excitement of actual power, he found the situation galling, and when he saw Carr about to imperil the whole structure of their joint success by throwing himself away on a vicious wanton he could not control himself. Scenes between the friends were so frequent that the quarrel became public property. One night, past midnight, Carr, coming back to his apartments in Whitehall, met Overbury in one of the galleries. "How now," he said, "are you up yet?" Overbury's corroding bitterness of soul forced him to pick a quarrel even at that unreasonable hour. "Nay, what do you here at this time of night?" he exclaimed. "Will you never leave the company of that base woman?" Overbury's servant, waiting for his master in the adjoining room, listened to the loud dispute in the gallery outside. He heard Overbury say, "Well, my lord, if you do marry that filthy, base woman you will utterly ruin your honour and yourself; you shall never do it by my advice or consent, and if you do you had best look to stand fast." Carr replied angrily: "My own legs are straight and strong enough to bear me up, but in faith I will be even with you for this!"—"and so parted from him in a great rage". He was not a tactful or even a prudent man, and in any case he was in love, and it seemed the natural thing to tell his mistress everything that concerned their prospects.

Frances Howard was now within sight of her great object. It was known that the king sympathized with her petition

Frances Howard, Countess of Somerset

for divorce, and that he regretted having given his encouragement to the marriage of two children. Such things, he said, could hardly prosper. He had caused an enquiry into the case to be set up, headed by the Archbishop of Canterbury. It seemed almost certain that with such backing the countess's petition would succeed; and then, it was well known, Carr would marry her, and she would be, after the queen, the greatest lady in the land, as she was already the most famous beauty. Three likenesses of her remain, made probably in the following year, 1614, when she was twenty. Two are prints, by Elstracke and Holl. The former, which shows her at full length side by side with Carr, is crude but extremely effective. The other shows her to the waist in medallion, labelled Vera Effigies Franciscae Comitessae Somersetiae. Both show the oval face, the large eyes wide apart, the short nose, small mouth and pointed chin, and in each it is the face of the typical juvenile delinquent: ignorant, sullen and resentful. In Elstracke's print the large eyes have a sidelong look which, with Carr's blankly smiling expression, suggests a strong likeness. More interesting still is the oil painting of the countess in the National Portrait Gallery, by an unnamed artist. This is the *portrait d'apparat,* while the prints have more of the qualities, realistic but limited, of a press photograph. The colouring is exquisite. The crinkled hair, turned back in a full, high cushion, is the colour of hair that has been fair in childhood. The skin is milk-white with a briar-rose pink in the lips and yet fainter pink in the cheeks. The eyes are the purest, darkest grey. But though the vulgar, soiled look of the prints is not there, the portrait is infinitely more alarming than they; it has a smile, slight but diabolical.

In the painting the clothes are of the characteristic Jacobean colours, black and lacquer red embroidered with gold. In all three pictures the bodice is cut unusually low, a deep oval showing the whole depth of the bosom, the sides just concealing the nipples. The scooped-out effect is not æsthetically beautiful, and combined with the rigid bodice and over-elaborate upholstery of the rest of the dress it gives an impression of deliberate lewdness. The fashion was not a general one and Frances Howard's use of it was commented on at the time. In *Truth brought to Light,* the author, describing her behaviour and Carr's at this period, says: "Yellow bands, dusted hair, curled, crisped, frizzled, sleeked skins, opened breasts beyond accustomed modesty with many other inordinate attires were worn on both sides to the show of the world." Vera Effigies shows the countess wearing a double rope of pearls hanging under her ruff between her breasts, and this seems to have been a favourite ornament of hers. Chapman wrote a poem about the happy issue of the divorce proceedings, called Andromeda Liberata. Andromeda was the countess, Perseus Carr, and the poet was set upon and cudgelled by some of Essex's friends because the conclusion could not be avoided that the monster was her husband. The poem indeed is a dull one, but it speaks of Andromeda's crystal breasts, "laid out", with pearls between them.

The commission of inquiry into the grounds for divorce opened in April of 1613, and the chairman, the Archbishop of Canterbury, was morose and reluctant about the business from the start. Dr. Abbot was a harsh and unsympathetic man, but he was transparently honest and he thought that there was something very much amiss with the attitude of the interested parties, including the king. He objected to being called upon to preside over such a case, and he was far from satisfied that every remedy had been tried—prayers, patience, medical advice—or that a long enough time had been allowed before such a drastic step was contemplated. This, however, was all he did suspect. He had no idea that the whole proceeding was an impudent farce. He told the king that he thought they should proceed with caution, and James, seeing at once where this attitude was likely to lead,

Frances Howard, Countess of Somerset

abruptly informed the archbishop a few days later that a commission had been appointed under the Great Seal and that the hearing would begin immediately. The commissioners included the archbishop, the Bishop of London, the Bishops of Litchfield and Ely, Sir Julius Caesar and Sir Daniel Dunn. They first took the evidence of the Earl of Essex. The earl had made up his mind to allow the charge, but he was determined that he would not be declared impotent and therefore unable to marry again. He allowed it to be understood that though he was not impotent in regard to other women, he was so in regard to his wife. When he was asked whether he loved her, he replied: "When I came out of France, I loved her. I do not so now, neither ever shall I."

On the countess's behalf it was said that no one could be sorrier than she; she had been willing, indeed anxious, to lead a normal married life and to be made a mother. The matter had disappointed and distressed her beyond words. Her statement was reasonable and convincing; its only flaw was that not a word of it was true. This, however, could not be known by any of the commissioners, by most it could not even be suspected; but they asked for a proof that the marriage was a nullity and a committee of ladies was appointed to see whether the countess were indeed a virgin. This committee included Lady Suffolk herself, five other great ladies of the court and two midwives. The countess asked that her face might be veiled while she underwent this examination and the bishops willingly allowed it. Some said that it was little Miss Monson who was sent in under the veil, a virgin so young that she could scarcely be anything else; others said that it was "a relation of old Kettle". At all events the verdict was satisfactory, that is to say, it was the right verdict; but Lady Suffolk at least must have known that the veiled girl was not her daughter and the fact would seem to have been suspected by other ladies. Lady Knevet exclaimed that she wished she had never been brought into such a matter and she cried for the rest of the day. The archbishop heard of this and remarked: "These things please me little."

The proceedings dragged on; the matter had at least clarified itself to this degree: the archbishop and the Bishop of London were quite clear that on principle the divorce ought not to be allowed, and the king was determined, by a mixture of abstruse argument and autocratic power, to get it through at all costs and as fast as possible. The laymen were courtiers and heart and soul at the king's disposal, the other bishops agreed with the archbishop, but were allowing themselves to be gradually suborned by the royal interest.

In the meantime Overbury's fate was closing over him. In April James offered him the choice of two diplomatic appointments, to France or to Russia. Overbury had no intention of leaving London, particularly at this crisis of affairs while he still hoped that, though the divorce could not be prevented, he might yet dissuade Carr from a marriage with Lady Essex. The concealed motives of the king, of Carr, of Overbury himself, make any comment on the bare facts rash and useless, but the facts themselves were not in dispute. Overbury refused the appointment and Carr supported him in his refusal, assuring him that, though the king would be angry, his displeasure would be only temporary. James took the refusal in very bad part and, saying that Overbury had been guilty of contempt, ordered him to the Tower. Carr again reassured his friend. The imprisonment, he said, was merely a gesture. It would be brief and some high promotion for Overbury was even then in store. In the electric atmosphere of the coming storm, the faculties of an experienced courtier were quickened to the power of prophecy. Sir Henry Wotton wrote to Sir Edmund Bacon: "Yesterday about six o'clock at evening Sir Thomas Overbury was from the council chamber conveyed by a clerk of the council and two of the guard of the Tower and there by warrant consigned

Frances Howard, Countess of Somerset

to the lieutenant as close prisoner ... now in this whole matter there is one main and principle doubt, which doth trouble all understandings: that is whether this were done without the participation of my Lord Rochester or no? ... These clouds a few days will clear. In the meantime I dare pronounce of Sir Thomas Overbury that he shall return no more to this stage." Sir Henry Wotton's prophecy was remarkable, but even he would not have foreseen that Overbury had not six months to live.

It is possible that the motives of the king and Carr were what they appeared to be. James, in Sir Henry Wotton's opinion, had long "distasted" Overbury. He disliked Overbury's haughty and domineering caste of mind, and he objected to the close intimacy and the mutual affection between him and Carr. When Overbury repulsed a royal favour with brusque incivility, James might well be glad of an opportunity to visit him with a spell of imprisonment. Carr had an even stronger motive for wanting Overbury to be locked up at present where he could do no harm. It was in Overbury's power to lay such information with the archbishop that Dr. Abbot would flatly refuse to continue the divorce proceedings. No threats of personal ruin would deter such a man as Abbot from a refusal once he knew the real facts of the case; and though he might be deprived of his mitre for it, the harm to Lady Essex would have been already done. To have Overbury shipped abroad would not lessen the danger. He could write letters even from Muscovy. The only safe course was to have him under lock and key where he could neither receive nor send letters without the knowledge of the gaoler. Carr may not have meant anything more than this. Though the suspicion against him is very strong, the verdict usually returned on his case is that there was little solid evidence against him.

There is no doubt whatever about Frances Howard. She was a murderess. The machinery which was to free her

Six Criminal Women

from Essex was already in motion, and the bare notion that Overbury might bring it to a stop roused all her formidable powers of initiative and ruthless determination. This was the mainspring of her action, but she had also that violent resentment of criticism which is perhaps part of the criminal's self-protection. Overbury had called her base, filthy and a whore. She sent for Mrs. Turner and poured out a torrent of indignant abuse of him so fierce that it would seem to have brought on a fit of hysterical crying. Mrs. Turner, infected by her hysteria, wept, too. The author of *Truth brought to Light* said that "there was such a storming between them as is incredible". The countess determined that Overbury should die; and determination such as hers can accomplish almost anything.

Dr. Forman was dead. He had died in a boat on the river, having foretold his death to the day; but Mrs. Turner was now in touch with a Dr. Franklin, a far less distinguished man but one perhaps even better for such a purpose. Franklin was knowledgeable in poisons; he said he understood the properties of rose algar, lapis constitis, cantharides, white arsenic, great spiders, aqua fortis and powdered diamonds, but he had not experimented with the latter, as it was too costly. The countess told him impatiently not to be a fool and gave him money to buy some forthwith. She was preparing the means of Overbury's death as far as she could, but she required the help of someone in a different sphere. Sir William Wade was the governor of the Tower and under him the prisoners would be safe at least from unauthorized cruelties. The Earl of Northampton, however, had an interest in Overbury's removal. When his great-niece should be married to the favourite the keystone would be placed in the Howards' triumphal arch—provided there were no potent influence at Carr's elbow to wean him away from the Spanish alliance. Such an influence as that might ruin everything.

Frances Howard, Countess of Somerset

Northampton represented to the king that Sir William Wade ought to be deprived of his office because the Lady Arabella Stewart had outwitted him and his subordinates and managed to escape from the Tower. Northampton managed without difficulty to get the king's consent to Wade's removal and to the appointment of a nominee of his own, Sir Gervase Elwys. Even more damning evidence of Northampton's guilt was the appointment as Overbury's keeper of a man called Weston; this creature had been apothecary's assistant to the late husband of Mrs. Turner.

The process of poisoning Overbury lasted intermittently over five months. At first Sir Gervase Elwys did not know what was doing. He met Weston carrying a dish in one hand and in the other a little phial of greenish yellow liquid. This was rose algar. There was no one about when Weston met the governor and he said: "Shall I give it him now, sir?" At first Elwys was genuinely surprised and shocked; he told Weston that he must not think of poisoning prisoners; but even as he said the words he began to see the web around him: Northampton, Lady Essex, Carr—and he said no more. He saw where his interest lay, and before long he was even in Lady Essex's confidence. He knew that she sent "tarts and potts of jelly" and sometimes wine for Overbury, as prisoners' friends were often allowed to do, and he knew that Overbury had begun to be very ill, that he had attacks of diarrhoea and sickness; but the prisoner's youth and the hardy constitution of all those who survived in the seventeenth century at all, enabled him for a long while to throw off these attacks. Lady Essex was becoming impatient. Elwys wrote her his excuses, saying: "This scab is like the fox; the more he is curst, the better he fareth." Some of the tarts which her ladyship sent were so strongly poisoned that as they stood on the table in the governor's kitchen they had already turned black and stank. Elwys prudently threw these away. Sometimes Lady Essex sent wine and tarts that were harmless. With some of these she sent a note to the governor saying that he might give them to his wife and children: "I was bid to say that there were no *letters* in them." This sentence of hers afterwards did Carr much injury. It was taken for granted that "letters" was used for "poison", and who should have bid her say anything except him? It was judged to be one of the few pieces of evidence directly incriminating Carr.

Overbury did not know at first, whatever he may have suspected later, that his sickness was poisoning; but as week after week went by with no visit from Carr, nothing but letters containing evasive promises, and no prospects of release, he began to suspect and then to realize beyond all doubt that he was in a trap and that Carr, of all people, had sprung it on him.

He had been lodged in the Bloody Tower, the squat square building on the water-side, almost opposite the Traitors' Gate. The first and second floors have fallen away, but there remain the square ground-floor chamber, the spiral of steep, sharply angled stone stairs up which Overbury went, the stone walls that surrounded him and the narrow windows from which the prisoner looked on to the Thames with its moving freight of free and active men. April turned to May, spring to summer and the protracted strain and exasperation of imprisonment were driving Overbury frantic. He wrote letters to Carr, in which his feelings poured themselves out like streams of molten lava. "Is this the fruit of all my care and love to you? Be these the fruits of common secrets, common danger? As a man you cannot suffer me to be in this misery; yet your behaviour betrays you. All I entreat of you is that you will free me from this place and that we may part friends. Drive me not to extremities lest I should say something that you and I both repent. And I pray God that you may not repent the omission of this my counsel, in this place where I now write this letter." For

Frances Howard, Countess of Somerset

an instant the gift of prophecy had descended upon him as it had descended upon Sir Henry Wotton. But the next moment his own sufferings occupied him to the exclusion of anything else. It maddened him to hear that while he chafed and raged in his stone room Carr was carrying on his courtship, with all his usual attention to dress and barbering. "Notwithstanding my misery, you visited your woman, frizzled your head never more curiously, took care for hangings and were solicitous about your clothes . . . held day-traffic with my enemies without turning it to my good; sent me nineteen projects and promises for my liberty, then at the beginning of the next week sent me some frivolous account of the miscarriage of them, and so slip out of town; and all this ill nature showed me by the man whose conscience tells him that trusting to him brought me hither," and a man, he added, who knew "that what he speaks and writes hourly is mine, and yet can forget him that sowed that in him and upon whose stock he spends". This was what galled him most, the callous, insolent ingratitude of the smiling, vapid creature into whom he had put life as a puppet master animated his doll. "What I found you at first, what I found you when I came . . . how many hazards I have run for you . . . what secrets have passed betwixt you and me; and then for the last part, how when you fell in love with that woman, as soon as you had won her by my letters, and after all the difficulties being passed, then used your own for common passages; then you used your own and never after but denied, concealed and juggled betwixt (me) and yourself . . . thereupon you made your vow that I should live in the court, was my friend . . . stayed me here when I should have been gone and sent for me twice on that day that I was caught in the trap. . . . All these particulars I have set down in a large discourse, and on Tuesday I have made an end of writing it fair and on Friday I have sealed it up under eight seals and sent it by a friend of mine whom

I dare trust. . . . I sent it to him and then to all my friends noble and gentle, men and women, and then to read it to them and take copies of it. . . . So then if you will deal thus wickedly with me, I am provided that whether I live or die, your nature shall never die, nor leave to be the most odious man alive." Overbury was to die already, but if he had not been, he would not have got out of the Tower alive after such a letter.

His parents were much alarmed at their son's imprisonment and they both came up from Warwickshire to London. Old Mr. Overbury waited on Carr and urged him to speak to the king on Overbury's behalf. Carr replied plausibly that the king was even now thinking of releasing the prisoner and to speak about the matter at this point would annoy His Majesty and cause him to postpone his decision. The unhappy and doubtful father was obliged to accept this reply, but Carr had not liked the interview and he determined to forestall any repetition of it from the victim's mother. Before Mr. Overbury could return to his lodging a letter from Carr to Mrs. Overbury had been delivered there: "Mrs. Overbury: Your stay here in town can nothing avail your son's delivery therefore I would advise you to retire into the country and doubt not before your coming home you shall hear he is a free man."

Meantime the slow murder went on. Weston at different times administered to the prisoner rose algar and sublimate of mercury; the countess sent tarts powdered with white arsenic instead of sugar, Mrs. Turner dressed partridges for him with a sauce in which cantharides was used instead of pepper. He began to be deadly sick. He came out in abscesses, lost all appetite and had a burning thirst. Sometimes after eating a poisoned dish he had "as many as three score stools and vomits, some mixed with blood". His brother-in-law, Sir John Lidcott, was at last allowed to see him and was dismayed at his state, his emaciation and weak-

Frances Howard, Countess of Somerset

ness, his burning hands. Overbury asked him in a hollow voice, "If Carr juggled with him or no?" Lidcott in all good faith said he thought not, and tried to soothe him. Shocked and alarmed as he was at Overbury's appearance, he had no suspicion of foul play at that time, for the king had allowed his own physician, Dr. Mayerne, to visit the prisoner. Dr. Mayerne saw him only once or twice, but he sent in a subordinate, De Lobell, to make routine visits. It was this, and the fact that neither of these doctors was afterwards examined or brought to trial, that added to the atmosphere of murk and suspicion with which the whole ghastly business was enwrapped.

At last, on September 14, De Lobell prescribed a clyster and then left the Tower. It was given to the patient by an apothecary's boy, who had been paid twenty pounds for his work. The fee might well be high, for the clyster contained sublimate of mercury. After a night of continual vomiting, Overbury's powerful constitution was finally overcome. He died early on the morning of September 15. It is against this background that the smiling portrait of Lady Essex should be viewed: the stone-walled room and the victim's condition; the agonies of vomiting, the faintness and thirst, the running sores; the endless weariness of feverish nights; the voice scarcely audible from exhaustion; the death in the dark hours of the morning without a friend, and watched by the man who, it is said, smothered his last breaths with a pillow.

The good news travelled fast. Before midday a letter came to Sir Gervase Elwys from Northampton:

"Noble Lieutenant—If the knave's body be foul, bury it presently; I'll stand between you and harm; but if it will abide the view send for Lidcott and let him see it to satisfy the damned crew." This was how the earl referred to the dead man's relations. At noon he sent Sir Gervase another letter, repeating instructions for a hasty burial in the Tower chapel. "If they have viewed then bury it by and by; for it is time, considering the humours of that damned crew that only desire means to move pity and raise scandals." This was the Howards' attitude to anyone who threatened to injure the family fortunes.

It seemed as if the attitude had been thoroughly successful. Overbury was dead and the divorce proceedings were drawing to a close. The king had sent the commissioners a message to say that when the final decision was taken all he wanted to hear was a plain yes or no. He did not wish them to give any reasons for their answer, "For of sermons," said His Majesty, "there would be no end." This seemed to Dr. Abbot the worst part of the whole bad business, but he saw that protests would be useless. He would content himself with recording his honest opinion, that the nullity had not been proved. The king foresaw this, and to make all sure he drafted in two more commissioners on whose votes he could rely: the Bishops of Rochester and Winchester. The latter's son, in consideration of his father's services, was given a knighthood, and was known as Sir Nullity Bilson ever afterwards.

On September 18, three days after her enemy's death, Frances Howard was freed from her marriage vows. Her wedding with her lover was arranged to take place in December, and three months were hardly sufficient for the splendid preparations. She was now to prove the truth of the Spanish proverb: "Life says, take what you like—and pay for it."

The wedding celebrations were glorious as befitted the state of the bride and bridegroom. Carr was already Viscount Rochester; the king now created him Earl of Somerset, that the rank of Frances Howard's second husband might not be below that of her first. In wealth, Carr was far superior to Essex. He was now the richest man in the country. In this year, observers calculated that he must have spent at least ninety thousand pounds. In modern money this would

Frances Howard, Countess of Somerset

be something approaching half a million. The presents he and his bride received were suitable to their wealth and state; the silver fire irons and coal scuttles, the gold cups and ewers and basins, the gold plate set with gems, and the sets of hangings the richest that had ever been seen, read like some tale of Aladdin's cave. The king's present to the bride was ten thousand pounds' worth of jewels.

The wedding was held at Whitehall on December 21, and the splendour of the setting was for once matched by the handsomeness and éclat of the bridegroom and the astonishing beauty of the young bride. For a bride to have her hair over her shoulders was a sign of virginity, and Frances Howard was married with her light, crisped hair "pendant almost to her feet". Some onlookers were divided between admiration at the lovely sight and disapproval of such impudent hypocrisy.

John Donne wrote an Epithalmion, and his verse gives the concentrated effect of torchlight, jewels and brilliant beauty on that night.

*Then from those wombs of stars, the bride's bright eyes
At every glance a constellation flies,
And sows the court with stars and doth prevent
In light and power the all-eyed firmament.
First her eyes kindle other ladies' eyes
Then from their beams their jewels' lustres rise,
And from their jewels, torches do take fire
And all is warmth and light and good desire.*

Conspicuous among the pale, rich bridal clothes, the diamonds and the embroideries of gold and silver, was a man dressed from head to foot in black. His clothes had no ornament of any kind, but, even so, his sombre suit had cost him eighty pounds. This was Sir Ralph Winwood, an aspiring statesman who hoped that he might get the post of Secretary of State which Cecil's death had left vacant, and who therefore paid court to the favourite at each opportunity. This sable figure looked ominous enough, but his behaviour was all generous kindness. In the course of the wedding festivities, which lasted a week, the king decreed that the bridal party should be entertained at the Merchant Taylors' Hall at the expense of the Lord Mayor and Aldermen. The procession was to go at night down the Strand and Cheapside, and the bride was to ride in the new coach which was part of the wedding paraphernalia. But Carr had no horses fine enough for such a show, and he asked Sir Ralph Winwood to lend the bride four of his own which were famous. Winwood replied gallantly that it was not for such a lady to make use of anything borrowed, and he begged as a favour that the Countess of Somerset would accept the horses as a present. Carr at first demurred on account of the great value of the gift, knowing no doubt that such presents are not made on the impulse of mere generosity, but he could not in the end refuse the superb offer, in accepting which he was no doubt urged on by his wife, and the procession received its final adornment in the four matchless horses that drew the bride's coach. Wilson says: "They all rode a-horseback into the city in the evening, . . . the men attending the bridegroom, the women the bride . . . so be-spangled with jewels that the torches and flambeaux were but little light to the beholders."

The final festivity was the most beautiful of all; this was the Masque of Flowers, presented by the young gentlemen at Gray's Inn, devised and also paid for by the Attorney-General, Sir Francis Bacon. His fellow lawyers had offered to share the cost of the production, but Bacon, anxious to maintain his high standing with the king, insisted on paying the whole two thousand pounds himself. Ben Jonson had contributed a charming little divertissement, "Challenge at Tilt", a conversation between two cupids on the perfections of the bride and bridegroom:

Frances Howard, Countess of Somerset

1st Cupid: Was there a curl in his hair that I did not sport in, nor a ring of it crisped that might not have become Juno's fingers? His very undressing, was it not love's arming? Did not all his kisses charge, and every touch attempt? But his words, were they not feathered from my wings, and flew in singing at her ears like arrows tipt with gold?
2nd Cupid: Hers, hers did so into his, and all his virtue was borrowed from my powers in her.

But Jonson's full-length masque for the occasion, to say nothing of the tedious one produced by Campion, were quite outshone by the radiant charm and originality of Bacon's.

The description of the garden-scene is fascinating, for it so clearly recalls Bacon's description in his essay on gardens. Two of the principal figures were Jove's messenger, Gallus, and Primavera. The messenger was dressed to suggest a game-cock, all in yellow with a small yellow hat, and on it a red feather like a cock's-comb, a carnation-coloured pouch at his side, and yellow boots with a long prick at the heel like a cock's-spur. Primavera wore the colours of spring, white, silver, yellow, gold and green. The audience were told that, whereas tales of antiquity described boys being turned into flowers, they should now see flowers turn into young men. The flowering bosquets parted, and thirteen young gentlemen of Gray's Inn came out to dance; they wore white trunks and doublets, white silk stockings and white satin shoes; the upper part of their costume was embroidered in flowers mixed with silver. Their pumps were fastened with flowers to match the flowers on their hats. Their white and silver gloves were presents from the bridegroom, the white and silver scarves tied above their right elbows were favours from the bride.

In these scenes of light and fragrance, colour, brilliance and music, Frances Howard at last achieved the height of her desire. Lust, ambition, revenge, were all completely gratified. There was but one drawback—she had an awkward number of people about her who pressed for money in a rather particular way. Mrs. Turner was truly devoted to her, and though she received a great deal of money from the countess, she was not to be reckoned as a potential danger. But Dr. Franklin was another matter. His demands were peremptory and they were also exorbitant. He required an annuity of two hundred pounds for life, and a cash payment of another two hundred, likewise half a crown daily for boat hire and ten shillings a week for board. He offered to bring in one of his relations to this profitable connection, saying that if his cousin had any suit that the countess's influence could secure, he, Franklin, would undertake to get it for him. He explained his position, only in part, but enough to make the cousin uneasy. "But, cousin, will God bless you for what you do in this?" Franklin replied: "Let them talk of God that have to do with him." Then there were two other purveyors of charms and potions whom Mrs. Turner had applied to on the death of Forman; they were Dr. Savories and Mr. Gresham. There was Forman's widow, who had possession of his properties and papers; there was Mrs. Turner's maid, "toothless Margaret", and the countess's own maid, Mrs. Horne; there was a young needy musician, Samuel Merston, who had been employed to carry a tart to the Tower, and slipping his finger under the crust to have a taste found that his nail was withered off. This curious experience had placed him, too, on the countess's already swollen pay-roll. But no one expects perfect felicity; some slight drawback will always be found in the most radiant fortune, and the countess was able enough and determined enough to deal with hers effectively, so far at least. As long as her position in the eyes of the world was unimpaired, she could put down anyone who threatened her more easily than such a person could injure Lady Somerset.

Frances Howard, Countess of Somerset

The two years that followed the wedding were all that Frances Howard, in a long life, enjoyed of real success. Yet even in this period the stain at the kernel of the fruit was spreading outwards towards the beautiful cheek. Carr, whatever the degree of his guilt in the matter, had ardently wished to be rid of Overbury, but now that Overbury was gone he found out what it was to have to do without him. He had, of course, secretaries, but no one who gave him that unique help and support on which he had relied more heavily than he knew. Since Cecil's death he and the king between them had done the work of First Secretary, but an appointment was now to be made, and the two leading candidates were Sir Thomas Laker and Sir Ralph Winwood. Northampton and Carr supported the former, but the king gave the appointment to Winwood. This was a sort of setback to which the Howards were not accustomed, and it was the first personal rebuff Carr had ever had since he attracted the king's favour seven years before.

It was not important in itself, but Carr was in a frame of mind to make much of it. James was still devoted to him and had he kept his head he need never have lost his place, but his situation was now one that needed more tact, self-control and common sense than Carr possessed. On the one hand, as a young man who had just made a marriage of passion, he spent most of his time with his wife, and made it plain that his attendance on the king was an irksome duty. On the other hand, when he felt himself slighted or that others were unduly favoured, he used his great intimacy with the king to burst in on him at unreasonable hours, often very late, when, after a storm of unkind and angry words, he would abruptly make away, and the king's indignant servants would know that their master was left to another sleepless night.

He had not the sense to remember that what a nervous man like James valued above all was emotional security.

James detested quarrelling and was afraid of violence. Once, Carr's youth and strength had been a buttress to the king against his annoyances and mishaps, just as the young man's beauty had been the delight of his existence. But now Carr did not care about pleasing and humouring him any more. The enormous wealth his favour had allowed Carr to accumulate had removed that urgent incentive to please which had once made the young man good humoured, sympathetic, affectionate. Now Carr found it exceedingly difficult to be pleasant to a man whose virtues, however great, did not interest him, whose personal habits were repulsive and who was continually making a fool of himself; it was especially difficult when such a man demanded the show of affection; such demands were enough to bring on a kind of nervous abhorrence. Carr had got to the point at which he could hardly bring himself to treat the king with reasonable civility. His position was very understandable. It was also very dangerous.

In March of 1615 the Earl of Suffolk, who had been made Chancellor of Cambridge University, entertained the king there. The large party was almost entirely confined to the Howard connections. There were very few ladies present except Lady Suffolk and her daughters Lady Salisbury and the bride, Lady Somerset. This was perhaps owing to the Howards' wish to keep it a family party, but the effect was unfortunate. It suggested to onlookers that other great ladies were cold-shouldering Lady Somerset and her mother.

Carr behaved with utter lack of judgment throughout. Considering the king's susceptibility to interesting young men, to take him to Cambridge was an act of madness; or, if the visit could not have been avoided, Carr should never have left the king's elbow. But the hospitality of the colleges was lavish and his bride was there to share the festivities with him. He was taken up with receiving ovations to himself and compliments on the fairy-like beauty of his wife. He

Frances Howard, Countess of Somerset

was only too ready to leave the king's society and enjoy his own grandeur and importance. Events fell out exactly as a shrewder man would have foreseen and feared. A Latin comedy was acted in Trinity Great Hall and there, standing about among other young fellows, was a youth named George Villiers, the son of a poor squire in Leicestershire. He was shabbily dressed, in "a black suit much broken out", and his beauty still startles us from the portraits of him by Van Dyck and Janssen. Those painted in his early youth when Villiers had just begun his career as favourite have an unearthly radiance like that of the morning star. The king called him Steenie after a picture in the Banqueting Hall which showed St. Stephen with the light pouring from his face.

Carr was so unpopular that once it had been seen that a new face had attracted the king there were many people of high eminence who were ready to back the new aspirant, to find him in money, clothes and jewels so that he could appear at court and allow his beauty to continue its work. When his patrons had bought Villiers the post of King's Cupbearer, Carr had grasped the fact that a potential rival to himself had at last arisen. Villiers at the time of his early portraits was clean-shaven; his face possessed a bony yet delicate contour, with enormous haunting eyes. He was extremely graceful, his hands were exquisite. It was this apparition clothed in white silk from head to foot that Carr was obliged to see, hovering in the king's view, standing beside his chair or kneeling at his feet. During one dinnertime a servant of Carr's threw a bowl of soup over this celestial creature. Villiers instantly struck him. The penalty for violence in the king's presence was severe; it meant imprisonment and might mean that the culprit's hand was to be cut off by the executioner. In the ensuing commotion Carr urged that this sentence should be carried out, but James, with characteristic subtlety, sent for the Archbishop of Canterbury to ask his advice as to what should be done. Dr. Abbot said that the incident was most regrettable, but he suggested that the king should overlook it this once.

The situation between Carr and Villiers made Carr increasingly bad-tempered. He had abandoned his use of charming methods and tried to maintain his position by domineering over what he thought was the king's weakness, but here he was mistaken. The king wrote him a very remarkable letter.

"What shall be the best remedy for this, I will tell you—be kind. . . . Consider, I am a free man if I were not a king. . . . If ever I find that you think to retain me by one spark of fear, all the violence of my love will in that instant be changed to as violent a hate. . . . Let me never apprehend that you disdain my person and undervalue my qualities; and let it not appear that any part of your former affection is cold towards me."

This seems to have had some salutary effect. So much of the old relationship remained that whenever Carr could make the effort the embers rekindled into a glow. Northampton died in this year, and in the consequent reshuffle of offices the king made the elder favourite Lord Chamberlain, saying that this post of such nearness to himself could only be fitly given to the man who was nearest him in affection. Carr still had his anxieties. He could never be entirely at ease again now that Villiers was there, and he was at feud with the Secretary, Sir Ralph Winwood. He had never forgotten that that appointment had been made against his own wishes. When he was supposed to be filling the Secretary's office himself, he had neglected it, but now that Winwood had it he used his position to interfere continually, overriding the Secretary's decisions and treating him with undisguised animosity. But on the whole, though he had something to bear, he had much to enjoy. He was still the

Frances Howard, Countess of Somerset

first favourite, he was Earl of Somerset, he enjoyed a wealth, a power, a celebrity unequalled in the kingdom.

Then the blow fell.

In June 1615 there died in Flushing an obscure young Englishman who had left his own country somewhat hurriedly two years before. If Frances Carr had ever laid eyes on him she could not have expected that injury could come to her from such a source. But before he died the young man relieved his mind by making a confession to the English consul in Flushing. He was the apothecary's assistant who had given Overbury the poisoned clyster.

This information was seen at once to have an extraordinary importance attached to it. The English consul decided to lay it with the Government forthwith. He sent it to the Secretary Winwood.

Sir Ralph Winwood could do nothing with it at first, except keep it. Then, as if the spark were creeping up the train towards the gunpowder, within two months this discovery put him on the track of a much larger one. Lord Shrewsbury asked him at a dinner party if he might recommend to his patronage Sir Gervase Elwys. Winwood said, By all means, only he would like first to hear Elwys's version of what had happened to his prisoner, the late Sir Thomas Overbury.

Sir Gervase Elwys, not clever at the best of times, and now thoroughly startled and anxious to stand well with the Secretary, gave a rambling account of how attempts at poisoning had been made and foiled by his own vigilance and attention to duty. Mrs. Turner's name was mentioned, and Winwood pricked up his ears. He saw the king, and James, after listening very carefully, ordered Elwys to submit to him a written statement of what he knew of Overbury's death.

Lady Somerset was staying at Henley in Oxfordshire and Mrs. Turner was with her. To so great a lady news was always brought by those who would be well paid for it. The countess and Mrs. Turner were very soon informed that Sir Gervase Elwys was being interrogated. The pangs of fright assailed them. Mrs. Turner sent at once for Weston from the Tower and set out from Oxfordshire to meet him. They met at the village of Hogston, and in a private room of the village inn they concerted their plans as to what they should say and what conceal if the matter went further. That summer was a time of sickening apprehension. The countess was pregnant, and Mrs. Turner remained faithfully with her. She said afterwards that she loved Lady Somerset dearly.

Sir Gervase Elwys in his statement had incriminated only Weston and Mrs. Turner, but the latter's connection with Lady Somerset was a well-known fact, and the direction in which suspicion was pointing was unmistakable. It has been said that had Carr still been the king's first favourite James would not have allowed the proceedings to go any further, but this is denied by those who point to James's particular abhorrence of murder and say that he would never have overlooked such a charge. At all events, the king ordered the Lord Chief Justice, Sir Edward Coke, to open an enquiry. Coke, exceedingly competent and formidably bad-tempered, had soon accounted for the subordinates. His investigation began in September. Mrs. Turner, Weston, Franklin and Sir Gervase Elwys were brought to trial one after another, and from a motley throng of witnesses whom Coke's energy had swept together a tolerably consistent picture of events was made out. As the importance of the case against Mrs. Turner was that it showed what incentive the countess had had for wanting to get rid of Overbury, the whole story was brought out of her traffic with Dr. Forman, her attempts to wither her first husband, her employing of charms and aphrodisiacs to gain her second husband. Mrs. Turner had secured from the widow of Dr. Forman some

Frances Howard, Countess of Somerset

of his incriminating properties and papers, but some had escaped her and Coke, who combined the ability of a lawyer with that of a first-rate detective, had secured some of them. There were produced in court parchments covered with mystic signs, and one labelled "Corpus" to which was fastened a little piece of a man's skin; there was a black scarf full of white crosses, and a lead image of a man and woman in the act of love. There was a small wax figure of a man, sumptuously dressed in silk and satin; this represented the favourite. The countess with her famous hair was represented by a wax figure of a naked woman, "laying out her hair at a glass". While these objects were being shown in Westminster Hall, the scaffolding on which part of the great crowd was seated emitted a deafening crack. It was thought at once that this showed the anger of the devil at having his toys displayed to the public. The crowd's consternation was so great that the uproar was not quelled under quarter of an hour.

The most revealing confession after Mrs. Turner's was Franklin's. He told of how Mrs. Turner had brought him to the countess to receive her instructions for preparing poisons, and how she had been especially particular that the poisons should have a lingering effect. When she had tried to induce Cunning Mary to poison the Earl of Essex, she had asked for a poison that would work at three or four days' length. She clearly thought that this would look more like natural illness than a violent attack that proved immediately fatal. He had procured some aqua fortis, and Mrs. Turner had given it to a cat. The wretched animal "pitifully cried for the space of two days and then died". "Aqua fortis is too violent," said the countess. What did he think, she asked, of white arsenic?

All four prisoners were condemned to death. Weston was hanged in October, and Mrs. Turner, Elwys and Franklin were hanged in November within a few days of each other.

Six Criminal Women

Dr. Whiting, the clergyman who visited the prisoners before execution, had very interesting interviews with Mrs. Turner and Franklin. The poor woman showed the stupidity which often accompanies a criminal strain. She had never thought to come to this; she had imagined that the power of the Somersets would save her from the law itself. "Oh, my Lady Somerset," she cried, "woe worth the time that I ever knew her!" She was urged by Whiting to say if she knew of any more concerned in the crime. She mentioned the late Earl of Northampton; she said all the letters Carr wrote to the countess before their marriage came under cover from Lord Northampton. She added at different times two irrelevant but interesting pieces of information: one was that she had heard that Prince Henry had been poisoned by a bunch of grapes; the other was that Carr spoke such broad Scots she could hardly understand him.

Frightened as she was, she showed some traces of a decent, affectionate nature. "Alas," she said, "that so many should meet with such ill fortune!" and she adjured Whiting never to let a child of his go to court, unless he would see its moral ruin.

A contemporary print of her kneeling upon the scaffold shows her wearing black with a loose black garment over her gown and a small black cap; but the hangman, with hideous facetiousness, had dressed himself in a large ruff and cuffs dyed with her famous yellow starch. From this day forward it was out of fashion.

Franklin's conversation with Whiting is extremely suspect because he had divined that Coke had a theory of his own about the existence of a vast popish plot; and thinking that his life might be spared or reprieved if he could hold out a promise of information about it, he made out that Overbury's death was but one spoke in a giant wheel. The death of Prince Henry, the miscarriages of the queen, were all matters on which he could claim to throw a light. As much of what he said is rejected it is perhaps not justifiable to say that the more interesting parts of it are true. Nevertheless, for what it is worth, he said that the countess could obtain plenty of money, as much as was wanted, but that she had not got it in her own possession, her mother gave it to her.

The public excitement was now immense and a sensation had been caused at the execution of Weston by a party of gentlemen, including Overbury's brother-in-law, Sir John Lidcott, riding up to the scaffold. As Weston stood with the rope round his neck, one of them called out: "Did you poison Overbury or no?" Weston replied, "You do me wrong at such a time." Then he said that he had left his mind with the Lord Chief Justice, but added, "I die worthily." Before he could be spoken to again, the hangman turned him off. The effect on the crowd of this dramatic interruption was that some great one or ones were behind the criminals so far brought to trial.

When Sir Edward Coke's enquiry was concluded he made out an indictment against Carr, summoning him to London. Carr was with the king at Royston when it was brought to him, and the shock, acting on the arrogance of seven years, made him lose his head completely. He exclaimed that Coke had no business to summon *him*; he would not go. James, with rare dignity, answered gently: "Nay! For if Coke summons me, *I* must go." He took an unusually affectionate farewell of Carr, kissing him frequently on both cheeks, and exclaiming how glad he should be to see him return. But Carr was hardly in his coach before the attendants heard the king say: "I shall never see thy face again!"

When Carr arrived in London he had a conversation with his wife, which can only be guessed at; but as a result of it he used the Privy Seal which was in his possession to empower a constable to break into an empty house where a box and a bag of letters had been left by Mrs. Turner. These he recovered and burned, but an equally incriminating collection escaped him. Sir Robert Cotton, Northampton's late secretary, also had a box of letters to the earl, from Carr and from Frances Howard, and he had entrusted them for safety to a Mrs. Farneforth, who had given them to her landlord. When at Cotton's demand she asked for them back, the landlord, alive to the suspicions that filled the air, refused to give them back without first seeing what they were. One look was enough. He sent the box at once to the Lord Chief Justice. The messenger found that Sir Edward was from home; he was at St. Paul's, "hearing of a sermon". The messenger went off to St. Paul's and caught the Lord Chief Justice as he was coming out. They retired into a vestry and Coke opened the box then and there. He had no cause to complain of ill luck in getting up his evidence.

Coke was extremely angry when he heard how Carr had abused the Privy Seal to destroy evidence against himself and his wife, and he ordered both him and the countess to be placed under restraint. Carr was confined in the Dean of Westminster's house, and his wife first in the Cockpit at Whitehall and then in Lord D'Aubigny's house on the river bank at Blackfriars. Their position was now acutely alarming, for they could neither consult with each other nor did they know what was being exposed by Mrs. Turner, Weston, Franklin and Elwys. But the countess's beauty and perhaps some private store of ready money procured her a little of her old influence. She got a note conveyed to Mrs. Turner who was then awaiting her trial and she managed to send a messenger to Westminster to let her know "how her lord did". Her passion, at least, had not yet drained itself away. Later a waterman was brought before Coke, for conveying a message to her. He was in his boat on the river when someone on the bank told him to knock with his oar on one of the windows overhanging the water and to hand in a letter when the window was opened. But apart from these

Frances Howard, Countess of Somerset

small means, the earl and countess had no communication with each other.

In December the countess was delivered of a daughter. It is said that after the birth she had laid a wet cloth on her stomach, having been told that this would kill her. Three months later, in March of 1616, her baby was taken away from her and she was sent to the Tower, where her husband was already a prisoner. She protested vehemently at being parted from her infant, but her wildest protestations were reserved for something else: she implored that she might not be lodged in the Bloody Tower, where Overbury had died. Sir John Key, who had replaced Sir Gervase Elwys, treated her kindly. He caused her to be placed in the Brick Tower, in the apartments that had been used by Sir Walter Raleigh.

Meantime, the king had fallen out with Sir Edward Coke, and the getting up of the case had been handed over to his great rival, Sir Francis Bacon. The last time Bacon had taken up his pen in anything to do with the countess it had been to devise the Masque of Flowers for her wedding celebrations. Though Bacon was a man of genius and Coke was not, Coke was the more distinguished lawyer of the two. But in this case Coke had been somewhat carried away by his obsession about a popish plot. In his immense zeal, he had impounded thirteen fortune-tellers and a piece of paper picked up in the fields after the death of Prince Henry, saying: "Now is the first branch cut from the tree." Bacon apologized for having this nonsensical stuff among the evidence, but, he said, it had been put in by Coke, "who will think all lost except we hear something of the kind". "Such it is," said Bacon, "to come to the leavings of a business."

In two months' time the Attorney General had done his work. The countess was to be tried first, and it was understood that her trial would open on May 18. London was crowded for the double event. People had come up from the country by the score, and though many of the nobility usually left their town houses for the summer, this month not a family but was in residence. Seats in Westminster Hall were fetching fancy prices. Five pounds for one seat was a common figure, and fifty pounds for a corner that might hold a dozen. To the intense chagrin of those who had paid so much, on the morning of the seventeenth it was announced that the trial had been postponed for another week. When the countess had been told that she was to appear on the eighteenth she had collapsed, and a short respite was given; as she was the centrepiece of the proceeding, it was worth the judges' while to wait till she could sustain her role with some calmness.

The trial opened at ten o'clock on May 24. When the Lord Chancellor, the Lord Chief Justice, the Great Seal, the Recorder, and the Attorney General, with their attendant officials, had taken their places, and the peers who composed the jury had all answered to their names, the Lieutenant of the Tower was ordered to bring in the prisoner. Everyone had heard of this famous beauty, but some of them now saw her for the first time. She wore a gown of black woollen material with a lawn ruff and cuffs, and her light hair was covered by a hood of transparent black gauze. When she spoke, her voice was low and timid, but her composure struck some critical onlookers as strange and unsuitable in her desperate plight, "more confident than was fit for a lady in such distress".

The Clerk of the Crown called out: "Frances, Countess of Somerset, hold up thy hand." She did not realize that this was simply a gesture to signify her presence. She held up her hand, and kept it in the air. At last the Lieutenant told her to put it down.

The indictment was read over, and as the story Bacon had pieced together was repeated, she became very pale. When Weston's name was mentioned, she held her fan

Frances Howard, Countess of Somerset

before her face and kept it there until the indictment was finished. When she was asked whether she was guilty or not guilty, she answered "Guilty", "with a low voice and wonderful fearful". Bacon then rose and made a speech in which he narrated the gist of all the evidence which had been extracted at the previous trials. The State Trials of the seventeenth century were scarcely trials as we understand them; they were rather a justification to the public of a verdict that had already been agreed upon and it was a recognized practice for the prosecution to abuse the prisoner at every opportunity. James, however, had sent word to the Attorney General that on this occasion he wanted there to be "no odious or uncivil speeches". Bacon's speech was a model of restraint and his handling of the prisoner whom he had magnificently complimented as a bride two years before and whom he was now sending to her death was worthy of the extremely difficult occasion. When he had asked for sentence of death upon her, she was invited by the Clerk of the Crown to say whether she could show any reason why the sentence should not be pronounced. She replied: "I can much aggravate but nothing extenuate my fault. I desire mercy and that the lords will intercede for me to the king." Her voice was so faint that only the Attorney General who stood nearest her could make out what she said. Bacon repeated it for the judges and the peers to hear. "The lady is so touched with remorse and sense of her fault that grief surprises her from confessing herself. But that which she hath confusedly said is to this effect: that she cannot excuse herself and desires mercy."

The Lord Chancellor then addressed her:

"Frances, Countess of Somerset, whereas thou has been indicted, arraigned and pleaded guilty, and that thou hast nothing to say for thyself, it is now my part to pronounce judgment: only thus much before, since my lords have heard with what humility and grief you have confessed the fact, I do not doubt they will signify so much to the king and mediate for his grace towards you; but in the meantime, according to the law, the sentence must be this: that thou shalt be carried from hence to the Tower of London and from thence to the place of execution, where you are to be hanged by the neck till you be dead, and the Lord have mercy on your soul."

Standing far back against the wall was a spectator, inconspicuous but not unrecognized. It was the Earl of Essex.

Carr had all along refused to plead guilty, and he had refused also to believe that the king would, when it came to the point, allow him to come to trial. Considering the appalling danger which surrounded him, his arrogant self-confidence was amazing. On the evening of May 24, however, when his wife had been brought back from Westminster Hall, condemned to be hanged, and no word had come to stay his own trial which was to take place on the morrow, he realized at last that his hour had come. His fury was unbounded. Sir George More told him of the next day's arrangements, but even then Carr would not submit. He shouted that if he went to trial they should take him there in his bed, that he would not be tried, that the king had assured him he should never be tried. Then in a climax of rage he exclaimed: the king *durst* not bring him to trial.

Among much senseless raving Sir George More picked out these words as really ominous. It was late in the evening, but he lost no time. He had himself rowed down the river to Greenwich where the king then was, and, arriving at the palace, "he bounceth at the back stairs as one mad". The servants told him the king was fast asleep. Sir George replied that he must be wakened up at once, and when the king was roused, his reception of the news showed Sir George that he had done well to come even at this hour of night. James's agitation was pitiable. He wept and shuddered and said: "On my soul, More, I know not what to do. Help me in

Frances Howard, Countess of Somerset

this great struggle and thou shalt find thou dost it for a grateful master."

What More and the king actually discussed, or if the matter were in fact discussed at all, was not, of course, stated by Weldon, who gives the account.[1] The secret which united the king, Carr and no doubt Overbury has never been revealed. Some declared that the king had been guilty of Prince Henry's death, but no serious support has ever been given to this theory and such a crime is entirely inconsistent with everything that is known of James's character. It is usually supposed that Carr was threatening to expose the fact that improper relations had existed between the king and himself; for though the fact cannot have been entirely secret, since it was known to some and suspected by many, yet this was not the same thing as having it announced by Carr himself in the middle of Westminster Hall. More soothed the king as far as he was able, and on his return in the early morning hours he managed to induce Carr into a state of acquiescence. It is thought that he had been empowered to tell the prisoner that so far as the verdict went it was a foregone conclusion, but that his life should be spared if he behaved himself at the trial. At any rate, it seemed that More, whatever his methods, had produced the necessary effect, but Bacon had been knocked up early and told of the night's happenings, and Bacon was taking no chances. He arranged that two servants should stand behind Carr, holding a cloak between them. If the Attorney General gave them a sign, they were to "hoodwink" the prisoner and carry him from the Hall, and the trial should go on without him. This arrangement was explained to Carr and no doubt had its use in assuring his docile behaviour.

The trial began at nine on the morning of Saturday, May 25. Like his wife, the prisoner appeared in black, a

[1] *Court and Character of King James I.*

black satin suit with a black gown over it. He wore rich gloves and the George hung round his neck. His beard had grown long, but it and his hair were curled as usual. It was noticed that he was pale and that his eyes were sunken.

It is generally held that Carr's connection with the murder of Overbury scarcely admits of doubt, but that the prosecution did not bring home his guilt as decisively as it would be obliged to do today to secure a conviction. The presumption of his guilt was very strong, and Bacon said: "If in all cases of empoisonment you should require testimony, you should as good proclaim impunity." In the cases of so secret a crime, presumptive evidence, provided it were strong enough, was deemed to convict. Of presumptive evidence there was enough and to spare; the whole dreadful story in all its windings was presumptive evidence of Carr's being accessory to the murder, but the pieces of solid evidence against him were few. One of them consisted of some letters which Northampton had sent him, saying that Northampton had the Lieutenant of the Tower completely under his thumb, and so long as Northampton were in town Carr need not trouble his head. The affair would go forward.

Though the trial covered the same ground as that of the day before, it gave a far fuller picture of events, and it was marked by several passages of brilliant oratory in Bacon's speech for the crown, in which he described the horrible nature of the crime and Overbury's agonizing death.

The proceedings lasted for twelve hours, and ended by torchlight. Many had fainted from the strain and heat before, at ten o'clock, Carr received sentence of death.

He was taken back to the Tower, and, though he knew the sentence would not be carried out, had he known what he was to undergo he might have asked that it should be allowed to stand.

For six years he and his wife remained together in the Tower, and during that time, whether soon or late, their

Frances Howard, Countess of Somerset

passion died and left them nothing. They did not love each other or like each other. Esteem was naturally impossible to them. Yet there they had to be, shut up with each other, shut off from the world which had meant everything to them, and in whose light they had originally seen and loved each other: the king's favourite and the court's most celebrated beauty.

In January of 1621 they were released on condition that they lived in a place appointed by the king. Grays was chosen for them, which the countess had not seen since the dreadful summer when Mrs. Turner brought the news that Sir Ralph Winwood was on their scent.

In this house the ceremonial of a noble family was kept up, but husband and wife had ceased to speak to each other. They came to the same table for meals, but they sat opposite each other in unbroken silence. Marcus Aurelius said: "For nowhere either with more quiet or more freedom from trouble does a man retire than into his own soul," but the souls of Robert and Frances Carr afforded them no refuge. He had been like the man in a folk tale, lured by the destroying spirit of the marsh. Fair, pale, glittering with marsh light, she had risen from her black depths, and when he leaned towards her she had whipped her arms about his neck and dragged him down to stifle in slime and darkness.

Her own fate was the worse of the two. She lived at Grays for eleven years, and died there when she was thirty-nine. Her illness was a disease of the womb, and the horrible condition to which she was reduced, acting on all she had suffered of disappointment and anguish, brought on a kind of mania. Once nothing had been too fine and fragrant for the setting out of her beauty. Now she took a perverse delight in her physical degradation. Arthur Wilson heard of all this and it gave him a deep satisfaction.

Carr's daughter was seven years old when they removed to Grays, and though the child must have known that there was something very odd about her parents' life she had no idea of the truth. When she was a young woman she read, in the library of a great house, a contemporary pamphlet describing her mother's history, and fainted away. The one living spot in Carr's ruined life was affection for this girl. When she was of marriageable age, the Duke of Bedford's son wanted to marry her. Their love was mutual, but the duke insisted on a dowry of twelve thousand pounds. The sum took the slender remains of Carr's fortune, but he said that her heart was set on the match and nothing should interfere with her happiness.

The extinction of his glories was complete, but James never forgot him. At intervals letters were exchanged, and once when Prince Charles and the all-powerful Villiers were out of the way the king sent for his former favourite to Royston. They met in the palace garden, and when the king saw him the old love and the old grief broke out of their hiding-place. He threw himself on Carr's shoulder and cried bitterly.

It is difficult to decide how much of Frances Howard's story was the result of environment and how much the result of a criminal mentality. Her circumstances were extremely unfavourable—a proud and selfish family, an immoral mother and a villainous uncle. But her own most amazing quality, her unconquerable determination, would have been dangerous in any milieu. It can seldom have been equalled in either sex. One of the extraordinary features of the story is its close interweaving of so many persons and interests. The passion of a girl of sixteen was the central theme, but it was repeated in a wild variety of love and hate, the hate being as fierce as the love. In a list which Sir Edward Coke made of his "Rareities" he notes a great diamond ring, "given by the queen to Sir Edward Coke, for discovering the poisoning of Sir Thomas Overbury".

JANE WEBB

Many people of great common sense reject with scorn the idea of planetary influence. At the same time it must be allowed that some subjects born under a particular aspect show in a marked degree those characteristics which astrologers would predict for them. As we do not know the year, still less the month, in which Jane Webb was born, we cannot know what planet was in the ascendant at her birth; but her character suggests that it was Mercury. Not only was she a snapper-up of unconsidered trifles, but the details of her career, scanty though they are, all suggest with surprising consistency that she was a Mercurial subject who had taken the wrong turning.

She was executed for picking pockets in 1740; and besides the trial which ended fatally, one other is recorded of 1738 as a result of which she was transported to Virginia; but the chief biographical matter concerning her was put down by the Reverend James Guthrie, a Newgate chaplain, who added to the monthly publications of the *Proceedings at the Sessions of Oyer and Terminer* a notice of the chief criminals hanged at the end of each Sessions. Guthrie's account, published in 1740, obviously achieved a considerable notoriety, for in 1745 it was published again as a separate pamphlet by another Newgate chaplain, the Rev. Mr. Gordon. The latter's account, for the most part, follows Guthrie's word for word, though it makes no acknowledgment. In places, however, he tones down his predecessor's version a little, and he also adds a good deal of new material. This is so full of small, graphic details, one conclude's either that it came from Jane Webb's own lips or that Mr. Gordon had the

Six Criminal Women

pen of a Defoe. He himself claims on his title page that the matter was taken directly from the criminal herself, and one is then left with the question as to why it does not appear in the earlier version. Two answers suggest themselves: one, that Mr. Guthrie thought the details of Jenny's goings-on as a debaser of the coinage would have made his account too long; this seems unlikely, as judging from his other biographical notices he was quite prepared to go to further lengths when he had anything to say, and as he wrote in the true catch-penny style, he would scarcely have omitted such sensational details if they had been known to him. The other and more likely theory is that Jane Webb did relate these facts herself, but not to Guthrie or to Gordon, who represented officialdom. Gordon's account gives the names of at least five men who were connected with her in criminal practices. She was entirely loyal to her associates, and one of her last cares was an attempt to establish the innocence of the woman who was caught with her in her last exploit. Possibly, therefore, Gordon collected this additional material after her death from members of her society who were then themselves in Newgate.

Her real name is a matter of doubt. Mr. Guthrie says it was Mary Young, but she also called herself Jones, Webb and Morphew. The fact that she almost always retained the Christian name of Jane suggests that it was her own. In Guthrie's words: "She got the name amongst her companions of Jenny Diver or Diving Jenny from her great dexterity in picking pockets." She is said to have been the illegitimate child of a lady's maid called Harriot Jones. She was presumably born in the first decade of the eighteenth century, and it must have been in England, for her unfortunate mother was delivered by Mother Wisebourne, who rose afterwards to great heights of elegant infamy, keeping a most recherché and scandalous establishment under the auspices of the notorious Heidegger, but who started in quite

Jane Webb

a small way in the humble district of St. Giles', in which phase of her career, no doubt, Jenny's mother was one of her clients. The infant was somehow or other got away to Ireland before she was five years old, and was brought up by an elderly female whom she called "nurse". This woman may have been self-respecting, though too many eighteenth-century tales of children's adventures suggest the contrary. At all events she took some pains with the little girl and "bestowed some small matter of learning upon her, as reading, writing and plain work". One significant detail emerges from this bald account of Jenny's childhood: by ten years old, she was "reckoned an extraordinary workwoman with her needle". The proofs left behind of the proficiency of eighteenth-century needlewomen, even of children, make us stare. The wonderful samplers with their rows of embroidered letters and figures, bordered by birds, flowers and arabesques, with the artist's name and her diminutive age, seven or eight years, perhaps, worked at the bottom, show how high a pitch of skill was attained in needlework when girls had very little else to do. It was a sort of national genius such as boys now show in anything to do with machinery. In each case the skill was encouraged by the demand for it in daily life. The man who has mechanical ability can earn his bread in a mechanized civilization. The girl of the eighteenth century who could sew and embroider well found a great demand for her work, even if it were poorly paid. Not only was every article of dress, every shirt, petticoat, nightgown and pair of stays, made by hand, all upholstery and household linen sewn by hand, but there was a vast field for the embroiderer, in men's coats and waistcoats, women's gowns, chair covers, quilts and curtains. The general standard was so high that a child who was "reckoned an extraordinary workwoman with her needle" must have been deft-fingered to a degree that was indeed remarkable. In Jenny's case it was an accomplishment that boded ill for the rest of society.

Six Criminal Women

Besides nimble fingers, Jenny had an aspiring mind, and by the time she was fourteen she had "an itching desire to see London". She had a young friend who was deeply attached to her and altogether under her influence. This was a lad who was manservant to a gentleman in the neighbourhood. Jenny knew that "nurse" would not allow her to set off on any escapade if she could prevent it, either from motherly care or because Jenny's services were expected to be profitable, and the problem before her was: "to get her clothes handsomely away", for even at fourteen Jenny was far too practical to run away without her little belongings. She proposed to the youth that they should run away together, and he was ready at the word and helped her to get her box down to the quay. She was already the guiding spirit, but when it comes to moving luggage any considerable distance a young lady of fourteen is at a standstill. The lad brought his own clothes as well and he had provided for the journey by robbing his master of eighty guineas and a gold watch. He at once gave Jenny ten of the guineas, which she put into a little purse of her own.

The voyage to Liverpool made Jenny very sick and she could not begin the journey to London without a rest. They therefore put up at an inn, and when she was recovered after a day or two they repacked their clothes and made arrangements to send their luggage by carrier to London while they themselves followed on foot: a mode of travel at once economical and interesting.

They went into the tap-room of another inn to refresh themselves before setting out, and most unluckily, for they had no sooner stepped inside than a man recognized Jenny's companion, having in fact pursued him to Liverpool on behalf of his late master. The alarm was given and the unfortunate boy was set upon. In the commotion his demure and childish companion was able to slip away unnoticed. She went into a public house near by, sat down and wrote

Jane Webb

her friend a letter full of artless sympathy for his ill luck, and promising to send his clothes when she got to London. Then the airy young creature set out by herself, as she afterwards said, "not in the least discomposed by the occurrence". The boy was sent back to Ireland, tried and sentenced to be hanged, but the sentence was afterwards altered to one of transportation. Jenny had not much warmth of heart, but she had a strange decency about her. She sent her friend his clothes as she had promised, and later she sent him his money, too.

In London Jenny fell in with an Irish woman called Ann Murphy, who gave her a lodging in Long Acre. Mrs. Murphy ostensibly made a living by taking in sewing. Jenny no doubt imagined that her talents as a sempstress had recommended her, but it might be that Mrs. Murphy, having sized up this spritely newcomer, had other views for her. At all events, orders for plain work did not appear to come in; and presently Mrs. Murphy said to her: "Jenny, trade being dead, suppose we was to take a new method of life, which at present you are a stranger to, but which I am acquainted with?" Jenny was agog to hear of the new method. "Why," said Mrs. Murphy, "if you will go along with me this evening you shall be instructed in this new art, but," she continued cautiously, "I must first swear you to secrecy, for fear, if you should not like it, you should discover." Jenny promised eagerly, and it became clear that what Mrs. Murphy had to propose was no new method as far as she was concerned, for she was a practised pick-pocket. That night Jenny acompanied her and her friends on a pick-pocketing expedition.

It seems to be a cardinal principle with thieves that the one who performs the actual theft must separate himself from the booty as soon as possible. The youthful Jenny was brought along on this occasion, not only to be instructed in the profession, but to receive the loot which the practitioners put into her hands as soon as they got it. The proceeds of this expedition were two diamond girdle buckles and a gold watch, which the gang disposed of for seventy guineas. Jenny's share was ten guineas only since her part had been merely "to stand Miss Slang, all upon the safe".

Very soon, however, she had learned all that the masters could teach and was instructing them herself. The pickpockets' trade in the eighteenth century was a thriving one, for since there were relatively few things to buy, such articles as there were were of costly materials and exquisite workmanship. The pockets of the well-to-do citizen of that day and of our own would make a strange contrast. The former had no fountain-pen, cigarette-case, lighter or torch, but he carried a snuff-box of solid silver or even gold, and his watch had cost anything up to a hundred guineas in money of the time, while his purse was heavy with gold coins. Buttons and shoe buckles were frequently set with diamonds, so were sword hilts. When pearl necklaces were worn, they were real ones, and diamond rings for both men and women were an ordinary part of full dress. The lucky thief could collect a fortune by a few weeks' work; but counter-balancing this state of affairs was the fact that the penalty of conviction for stealing any object worth more than five shillings was death. True, the law was sometimes strained in favour of the prisoner. In a case heard before Lord Mansfield, the plaintiff was urged to say that a stolen ring was not worth more than five shillings. He exclaimed indignantly that the setting had cost more than that. "The fashion alone was worth twenty shilling!" "God forbid," said the judge, "that we should put a fellow creature to death for fashion!" Johnson and Fielding were among those who complained of the insane harshness of the law that, in Johnson's words, at regular intervals "emptied the prisons of the city into the grave", and, as Fielding said, "carried cartloads of human beings to slaughter every few weeks". But such protests

Jane Webb

were contrary to the settled conviction of society as a whole. Men, women and even children of twelve years old were hanged for a wide variety of offences of which theft was the most frequent. The number of capital crimes in 1800 was over two hundred. Besides the extremity of the penalty if caught, the thief was faced with appalling conditions if he remained in poverty. The slums of eighteenth-century London were perhaps the darkest ever known, for the congestion of the urban areas had already developed while any scheme of state philanthropy was unborn. Hogarth's pictures of rags, vermin and emaciation in "The Idle Apprentice", "Gin Lane" and the "Frosty Morning" give one some idea of the sufferings which charitable men and women attempted to relieve piecemeal but which society accepted as part of the natural order. Johnson calculated roughly that a thousand people starved to death in London every year. What with freezing, starvation and disease, the prisons themselves, frightful as they were, had few terrors for the inhabitants of an eighteenth-century slum, and the risk of the gallows was no deterrent from a course that might bring in a handful of guineas—wine, meat, fires, fine clothes and a good bed. The natural result of such extremes was that the thief spent his money as fast as he got it, but Jenny's unusual temperament rose superior to the drawbacks of her situation. Cool, adroit, light-hearted and determined, she showed not only a technical brilliance that soon put her at the head of her profession, but a self-control and a constructive ability that enabled her to get solid benefit from her way of life.

When she had been initiated into the art of picking pockets, "finding money came in pretty fast this way", she decided to adopt the profession, and she prepared herself for it in a serious and business-like manner. A member of the gang who admired her came every day to give her lessons and to teach her the cant of the thieving fraternity. This had a word for every verb and noun likely to be used by the thief in his occupation. A few terms have passed into the language, such as "fence" for receiver, "bunce" and "blunt" for money, but the greater part of this curious language has disappeared, unless indeed it may survive in the underworld. The fact that Fielding when he used some of the words in *Amelia* gave translations of them, showing that the polite reader even of the seventeen-forties was not expected to be familiar with them, may suggest that the language exists still below the level of educated society. Some of the words and phrases still discoverable have an obviously picturesque origin, such as "tail" for sword, or "glim star" for jewelled ring. "Feme" for hand, "ridge" for guinea and "bung" for pocket are obscure in origin. Some were obsolete words used only in the cant; "lower", used for purse, is an archaic term for hire or reward. Most interesting of all are the words imported from other European languages, showing that on this level of society there was much more infiltration of foreign words than in the upper levels: such terms as "loge" for watch (horloge), "froe" for woman (Frau), "saweer" for find out (savoir), and "kinchin" for child (Kindchen).

The intimacy of these lessons, to which Jenny devoted two hours a day, resulted in her becoming her tutor's mistress. She told Mr. Guthrie that the connection was founded on the "great respect" which the parties entertained for each other. The words are ludicrous, but they convey an interesting impression. They suggest that Jenny, at least, had no passion. It would have been inconsistent with what we know of her character if she had.

Though she was not a person of much feeling herself, she inspired a good deal in others. She had already made two useful conquests, of the poor, devoted footboy and the expert thief. These were of an amorous nature, but in less than two years, by the time she was seventeen, she was held in admiration and respect by the whole of Mrs. Murphy's gang. She

Jane Webb

had, they recognised, every quality necessary for success. Her natural elegance and her taste for fine clothes—not at all the same thing as a fondness for heaping them on her back—enabled her to mix in throngs of fashionable people without arousing the least comment or suspicion. One of her early exploits illustrates this. The eighteenth-century fondness for listening to sermons made a church or tabernacle almost as good a hunting ground as a theatre. One day Jenny, looking the fine lady all over, joined the crowd surging upon the doors of the meeting-house in Old Jewry. Her sharp glance had lighted upon "a very great beau" whose dress was completed by a fine diamond ring. At the threshold the crush was greatest and the charming young lady held up her hand above the heads, imploring assistance. The beau immediately stretched out his own towards it. The gang pushed forward violently, and Jenny gripped his hand in her alarm, then her nerve seemed to fail her. "'Tis useless to try to enter!" she cried. "I will come another day!" and turning about, made her escape from the jostling mob. Once he was inside the hall, the gentleman realized that his diamond ring was gone. It was in vain to set up a hue and cry; the crowd still pouring in had placed an impassable barrier between him and the fair thief.

This skill in legerdemain Jenny developed to its fullest extent. She found a workman to make her a pair of false arms which could be folded in front of her. The crude appearance of the false limbs we are accustomed to see, and the staring production of modern waxwork, give us no idea of how skilful the old artists were. We may gather some from those wonderful waxworks of the seventeenth and eighteenth centuries still preserved in Westminster Abbey, and from the fact that plays and novels, such as *The Duchess of Malfi* and *The Mysteries of Udolpho*, depend for some of their action on waxworks being mistaken for human flesh, an effect which the modern additions to Madame Tussaud's could never hope to achieve. Jenny's false arms, when folded before her, deceived people sitting beside her in a church pew. With two pillows under her skirts and her arms folded across, she presented a convincing picture of a careful creature far advanced in pregnancy. In this guise she attended the Old Jewry meeting-house once more; her lover, dressed as a footman, had gone before to spy out who would be worth sitting next, and had detected two handsomely dressed elderly ladies with gold repeating watches at their waists. He carefully ushered his mistress into their pew, and others of the gang took the pew behind, to receive the plunder when the accomplished Jenny should have secured it. After the service, the ladies discovered the loss of their repeaters and were both outraged and bewildered. No one had been near them but the pregnant woman, and she, as everyone pointed out, and as they knew themselves, had never moved her hands from her lap during the whole service. Meantime, Jenny had disappeared nimbly and "delivered herself of her great belly", and now rejoined the tail end of the congregation as it came out, that she might assist "with the helping off of any more movables".

This was the feat that established her as the mistress of the gang. They were so much dazzled and enchanted by her daring and success that they unanimously chose her as their leader, the organizer of their work and the administrator of their share-outs.

Jenny devised the following rules for their society. They are probably much the same as those laid down by any successful leader of a gang; and her ability was shown, not in creative policy, but in the sense with which she recognized that these rules were good, and the personal influence by which she ensured that they were obeyed.

(1) No new member was to be admitted without the consent of the whole company.

Jane Webb

(2) No one should presume to go on any expedition on his or her own account, on pain of being entirely turned off and left to shift.

(3) That any new member should be a month upon trial, and that all that time they shall be instructed at convenient seasons in the cant tongue, so that they may speak to be understood only by the gang.

(4) That if any of the gang should happen to be taken up ... the rest shall stand by him or her and forswear anything to get such released, and, if convicted, a sufficient allowance to be given him or her in prison out of the common stock, that they may live in a genteel manner.

In some ways, this thieves' charter is much in advance of the laws of its time, for it is entirely democratic and makes no distinction between men and women.

The rest of the gang were the auxiliaries, without whom Jenny's various feats could not have been carried out; but the masterpieces of audacity and deception were performed by her, and the followers regarded her as a past mistress whom they were proud to follow. For one thing, she was no Jonathan Wilde, setting subordinates to rob on the highway while she stayed safe at home and took the greater part of their gains under threat of informing on them. Jenny herself was always in the part that carried the most risk, while the subordinates at work on the outskirts of the crowd had a very good prospect of escape. One day a dense crowd was expected in the London streets for the king's visit to the House of Lords. St. James's Park was thronged and the congestion was great in a narrow passage leading from the Park to Spring Gardens. Suddenly the crowd heard warning cries and the passers-by were halted by a commotion round a pregnant lady who had fallen down in the pangs of labour. Various sympathisers stooped over her to lift her up, but she seemed to dread movement and begged to be allowed to lie where she was for a little. Her nimble fingers removed one or two purses from her would-be helpers, and by the time she felt equal to getting up and going on her way her assistants had worked the crowd pretty thoroughly. The haul on this occasion was a heavy one: two diamond buckles, a gold watch, a gold snuff-box and thirty guineas in solid coin. When it was to be disposed of, Mrs. Murphy suggested that, as an announcement had been put in the papers offering a reward for the return of the articles and no questions asked, the offer should be closed with. Whereupon Jenny started up, and exclaimed, "By no means!" She said that, notwithstanding the promised indemnity, whoever took the property to the appointed place ran the risk of being "smoked" and "blown upon". It would never do. They must content themselves with the money their fence could procure for them. This was Mr. Roger Johnson who always acted for Jenny. He used to take the property over to Holland.

Jenny's objection to the practice of advertising rewards for stolen property and no questions asked was shared by an even more distinguished authority. Fielding, who was a London magistrate from 1749 to 1754, published in 1752 his pamphlet, *An Inquiry into the Causes of the Late Increase of Robbers*, and assigns this very practice as one of them. "If (the thief) hath made a booty of any value, he is almost sure of seeing it advertised within a day or two, directing him *to bring the goods to a certain place where he is to receive a reward* (sometimes the full value of the booty), *and no question asked*. This method of recovering stolen goods by the owner, a very learned judge formerly declared to have been, in his opinion, a composition of felony. And surely if this be proved to be carried into execution, I think it must amount to a full conviction of that crime. But indeed, such advertisements are in themselves so very scandalous and of such pernicious consequence, that if men are not ashamed to own they prefer a gold watch or a diamond ring to the good of the society, it is pity some effectual law was not contrived to prevent their giving this public countenance to robbery for the future." Fielding thought the victims ought not to advertise, and Jenny thought they ought not to be attended to if they did; there Fielding and Jenny were at one; but Fielding was also extremely severe on Mr. Johnson and his colleagues. "It is a very old and vulgar but very true saying" that if there were no receivers there would be no thieves. "Indeed, could not the thief find a market for his goods, there would be an absolute end of several kinds of theft: such as shop-lifting, burglary, etc., the objects of which are generally goods and not money . . . but at present . . . the thief disposes of his goods with almost as much safety as the honestest tradesman." It seemed to the anxious magistrate that the criminals enjoyed a preposterous degree of safety, but naturally it did not seem so to them. Their safety was that of a tight-rope walker who does not expect to fall but who knows that certain death awaits him if he should. Mr. Gordon said of Jenny's fraternity: "These people only date their lives by sessions and not by years, often saying, If I get over the next session, I shall do so and so." It was this situation which made Jenny's coolness such an inspiration to her followers and procured her their almost fanatical admiration. Her closest associate in these exploits was her lover. He seems, like the rest of the gang, to have had no reluctance to playing the part of her servant in public and usually accompanied her dressed as the footman of a fashionable woman.

One day Jenny became indisposed outside a handsome house in Burr Street, Wapping. Her footman knocked at the door and said to the maid that his mistress was "a little out of order"; might she come in and speak to the lady of the house? A kind answer was returned, "so directly in goes Jenny, grunting and groaning like one half-dead. Down comes the mistress and sends the maid upstairs for a chamber pot while she went to fetch the smelling bottle". Jenny and the footman were by themselves for a few minutes, in which time Jenny opened a chest of drawers and pulled out "a rich suit of clothes worth sixty guineas", which she rolled up and stowed into a special receptacle which she carried under her hoop. The maid now came back with the pot, and the footman, "out of decency, was desired to walk downstairs till his mistress needed him". The lady next bustled in and "was very busy holding the smelling bottle to Madame's nose". Jenny was seated in her chair, "in a very melancholy posture", and as her hostess stooped over her, with the maid looking on, Jenny contrived to get the lady's purse out of her pocket. The dexterity of this feat is almost unbelievable, but we have evidence of the same sort of thing within living memory. A barber tells us that he was once shaving the conjurer Giovanni, who presently said to him: "Anything the matter with your trousers?" Looking down, the barber found that his braces had been removed.[1]

Meanwhile, below stairs the footman had made a collection of silver spoons, silver salt cellars and silver pepper castors. He was now summoned upstairs and told to fetch a coach for his mistress who wanted to be at home as soon as possible. Jenny took leave of her hostess with the utmost gratitude and politeness and while the footman bawled up to the coachman the address of an eminent merchant in Tower Street, Jenny begged the lady to call upon her whenever she should be in that neighbourhood. The coach drove off, and at the end of a few streets, Jenny pretending she could not "ride easy" in a coach, the footman stopped it and paid off the driver. Thus was accomplished another tour de force, but the robbery of the unsuspecting lady must at last have been discovered, and as Jenny had performed similar feats in other parts of the town (and the town itself

[1] *Sunday Chronicle*, January 9, 1949.

Jane Webb

was not large) the victims gradually became known and talked of, and finally Jenny began to see her exploits related in the newspapers. Unlike many criminals, she knew when to stop. She had in any case no need to take unwarrantable risks. In less than three years the gang, besides their living expenses, had received three hundred pounds apiece.

Unwilling to attract any more attention in London for the time being, Jenny and the gang decided upon "a progress" down to Bristol where the Great Fair was being held. Jenny and Ann Murphy appeared as wealthy merchants' wives, two of the men as well-to-do dealers and the rest of the company as their servants. Many of their feats were decided upon impromptu, and their success depended, of course, upon their being able to catch each other's meaning and come in behind each other's efforts. Not only were they thoroughly versed in their secret language and their code of signs: their intimacy seems to have developed something like telepathic communication. In Guthrie's words: "They had their lessons so perfect, each knew one another's meaning by a nod."

One day at the fair they saw a West Country merchant who had just concluded a bargain, hand his servant a bag containing a hundred pounds, and heard him tell the man to go home, lock up the money in the escritoire and bring back the key to his master at the Fountain Tavern in the High Street. When the fellow had gone a little way, a respectable servant overtook him and said that the merchant had just made a bargain with his own mistress, a very rich lady, and now wanted his servant to bring the money to him at the lady's lodging. The poor creature at once complied. As they went, the footman expatiated on how rich and liberal his mistress was, and by artful conversation got his master's name from his fellow servant without the latter's seeing what he was about. At the lodging they found Jenny.

Six Criminal Women

"Who is this honest man?" she asked.

"Madam," said her footman, "it is Mr. S.'s servant."

Jenny at once made him welcome and told him that his master would be with them almost at once. In the meantime, all affability, she pressed a glass of wine upon the yokel, who was at first too bashful to accept it, but, having drunk it off, consented to take another, to his master's health, and a third, to Jenny's, with increasing confidence. The footman was now told to take the visitor into the next room to await his master's arrival. The good man began to feel drowsy, and this was not surprising, since each glass of wine had contained some drops of liquid laudanum. Presently he was fast asleep. Jenny and her confederates removed his bag and then left the premises themselves, telling the servants as they passed that the good fellow inside was very weary, and asking them to let him have his sleep out.

All in all, the proceeds of the Bristol tour were: living expenses for the whole company and thirty pounds apiece.

When they got back to London it was seen at once that their holiday had not unfitted them for work. A few days afterwards, about five o'clock in the evening, several of the gang, handsomely dressed and with an appearance that invited every confidence, were mingling with the throng going over London Bridge. There was a sudden congestion of carts and coaches, causing a flurry and commotion among the foot passengers, and a lady, unaccompanied, drew herself into a doorway for shelter. A well-dressed man took her by the arms and gently pushed her backwards into the doorway, screening her with his person from the tumult in the roadway. While the lady's arms were thus held in front, Jenny and an accomplice glided behind and cut off her pocket. When it was safe to venture out again, the lady thanked the gentleman for his care and made a fine curtsy before she walked away. In the pocket she left behind were thirty guineas, a gold snuff-box that fetched six guineas more, and

Jane Webb

a case full of silver instruments. The next day, "being upon business at the corner of Change Alley", one of the gang got a pocket-book containing banknotes for two hundred pounds. These went at once to Mr. Johnson, who gave a hundred and thirty pounds in ready cash for them.

Though Jenny could find scope for her art in almost any milieu, it was always recognized that the crowds coming out of theatres were the pick-pockets' special province. Jenny now took "a genteel lodging" near Covent Garden, that they might be conveniently situated for the playhouses. One night the gang "dressed Jenny up very gay like a person of quality" and she took a sedan chair and had herself carried to Covent Garden playhouse. Here she occupied a seat in one of the front boxes, and her gay, charming figure attracted the notice of an amorous young fellow with plenty of money and not much experience of London, being down from York. Jenny found there was nothing to be done in her line while the play was still on, so she left before it was over, and downstairs she was joined by the young spark. The famous Rose Tavern stood at one corner of Covent Garden, and he entreated her to come there with him and drink a glass of wine before she went home.

"'Sir,' says she, 'it is what I don't care to do,' but added with a sigh, 'If I thought you was a man of honour, I durst venture to drink a glass of wine, for sure there is no harm in that, but I am told there are so few men of honour—it is hard trusting.'" The enamoured young man assured her that he was the very soul of honour, and over their glass he made arrangements to seduce her at the earliest opportunity. The artless Jenny said that her husband would not be at home till very late the next evening, and if her new friend liked to call, that would be a convenient time.

When she got home, she was vehemently upbraided by the gang who had expected to meet her when the audience came out. Without her they could do nothing; in the whole evening they had taken but one gold snuff-box. Jenny, however, soon pacified them by what she had to tell.

The next night the gentleman presented himself at the appointed time. "He came dressed very gay, with a gold watch in his pocket, a gold-hilted sword by his side, a diamond ring upon his finger and a gold-headed cane dangling in his hand." He was received by two of the gang in rich liveries, who conducted him to his lady's waiting-woman, Ann Murphy, handsomely dressed, who in turn ushered him into the luxurious apartment where Jenny waited for him. Presently one of the servants brought up a bottle of wine and some delicious sweetmeats. The gentleman was agreeably surprised to find that his acquaintance was a woman of such quality. After civil preliminaries, he pulled off his clothes in a hurry, while Jenny, who was bashful, took off hers more slowly. The impatient lover jumped out of bed to help her and stooped down to pull off her shoes. Jenny grasped his hand to push it away and when she withdrew her own it had his diamond ring in it. They had no sooner got into bed than a fearful commotion at the door announced that the husband had returned. Jenny leapt to the floor, huddled on her nightgown, and, exhorting the gentleman to pull the clothes over his head, said that she would tell her husband she was ill and persuade him to sleep in his dressing-room, then when all was quiet she would return. Meantime she gathered up her lover's clothes, cane and sword and carried them out of the room to conceal them. She turned the key after her.

It was not till the early hours of the following morning that the gentleman brought himself to ring the bell. It was answered by the proprietors of the house who had to break down the door to get in. Like some band of malicious fairies, Jenny and her retinue had vanished into thin air, leaving only angry and bewildered mortals behind. The people of the house, on discovering that their elegant lodger and her

Jane Webb

servants had levanted, leaving their considerable bill unpaid, seized on the luckless gentleman who, without clothes or money, was quite at their mercy. They refused to let him send to his house until he had undertaken to discharge Jenny's score. The gang were thus beholden to him for several days' board and lodging of a most superior kind, while the proceeds of his diamond ring, gold-headed cane, gold-hilted sword and gold watch were two hundred and fifty guineas. Jenny's share of this was seventy guineas, but as usual one tenth of the entire proceeds was put by to finance the gang in time of difficulty.

Such an episode leads one to a consideration of the very curious case of Jenny's namesake in *The Beggar's Opera*. Was Jenny herself called after the Jenny Diver in MacHeath's troop of doxies or was she so celebrated by 1728 that Gay introduced her by name to give verisimilitude to a scene of low life? The introduction of living characters by name was not unknown in the theatre. Dryden made the Emperor Aureng-Zebe the hero of a play during the latter's lifetime. It is true that the Emperor was in India and Dryden was in Drury Lane,

"*Where half the convex globe intrudes between*",

but Gay would not have cared for objections from such as Jenny, even if she had been likely to make any. As Guthrie, who took down the information from her own lips, says that she got the name from her skill in diving into pockets, it seems fairly well established that she was not called after the girl in the opera. Such a circumstance, if true, could hardly have failed to be mentioned in their conversation. If that be accepted, then the description of Jenny in *The Beggar's Opera* is particularly interesting as a portrait, at least in general outline. MacHeath says to her: "What! and my pretty Jenny Diver, too! As prim and demure as ever! There is not any prude, though ever so high bred,

Six Criminal Women

hath a more sanctified look with a more mischievous heart. Ah! thou art a dear, artful hypocrite!" while Mrs. Coaxer observes: "If any woman hath more art than another, to be sure, 'tis Jenny Diver. Though her fellow be never so agreeable, she can pick his pocket as coolly as if money were her only pleasure. Now there is a command of the passions uncommon in a woman!"

Jenny may have been in prison before 1738, but in this year she was sadly caught, in a manner which reflected no discredit on her powers. On April 4 there was to be a festival of music at St. Paul's, and, a great crowd being anticipated at the coming-away, Jenny and the gang were industriously at their posts. Two ladies, Mrs. Rowley and Miss Reed, thought they would avoid the worst of the crush by going through Cannon Alley into Paternoster Row; but in the Alley the crowd was thicker than ever, and all at once Mrs. Rowley felt a hand under her hoop. She cried out: "What! Are you picking pockets here?" Jenny's mercurial agility would have carried her safely out of such a situation. Unfortunately, what could neither be foreseen nor helped, was the fact that a gentleman named Mr. Addy had been amusing himself by looking down on the throng from an upper window. He ran down at once and made his way to Mrs. Rowley, assured her that he had detected the thief, that he knew her for a famous pick-pocket, and that if Mrs. Rowley would prosecute he would give evidence. He ran off after Jenny and came up with her as she was in the act of picking the pocket of Dr. Best's lady. For once the darting fish was securely in the net. Jenny was taken before the Lord Mayor, committed to Newgate, and on April 11 came up for trial at the Old Bailey.

The gang had made desperate efforts. Some of them had visited Mr. Addy and offered him fifty pounds to drop his evidence. This proved unavailing. A row of seemingly respectable witnesses was produced: Ann Carter, Mary Cherry,

Jane Webb

Frances Fletcher, Mary Robes, John Taylor, Thomas Welch —all of whom swore solemnly to the prisoner's virtuous character, but in vain. Mr. Addy's evidence was fatal. He said that he had known Jenny by sight as a famous pickpocket these five years; that on April 4 he had watched her for two hours with a couple of her companions, bustling about and picking pockets as fast as she could. When she made the attempt on Mrs. Rowley under his very window his public spirit could tolerate it no longer and he had gone down to interfere. Jenny was convicted and, with thirty-seven other criminals, was sentenced to transportation.

For two months, until the batch of convicts of which she was one should be despatched, Jenny remained in Newgate.

The horrible condition of eighteenth-century gaols, which had aroused concern as early as 1729, when Oglethorpe's commission was appointed to enquire into it, was fully revealed by John Howard's exposure, *State of the Prisons in England and Wales*, 1777. Some of the worst distresses from which the prisoners suffered, as Mr. B. M. Jones explains in his brilliant work, *Henry Fielding, Novelist and Magistrate*, arose from the fact that gaols were originally places of detention only and not of punishment; that the latter was carried out by such methods as flogging, branding, or exposure in the pillory. The gaoler had no responsibility to feed the prisoner or to keep the prison in repair. His only duty was to see that the prisoner did not escape. Hence the loading of the prisoner with fetters, which made escape impossible even though the gaol might be so ruinous that it barely afforded protection from the weather. Guthrie himself tells of a prisoner whom he visited in an extremity of suffering from the swelling of his legs in their fetters and from intense cold. A few days later this man was found to have died in his cell. Sometimes the prisoners lay on straw, sometimes on the bare flags. It was no one's business to provide a bed, or any means of warmth. The parish provided a ration of

Six Criminal Women

bread to prisoners, and this had been fixed in Elizabeth's reign at a penny loaf a day. In the sixteenth century the penny loaf weighed twenty ounces, in the eighteenth century it weighed nine ounces, but the ration was still the penny loaf. The difference between reasonable comfort and an approach to death from exposure and starvation was bridged by what the prisoner could pay. "The gaolers avowedly lived by the fees extracted from the prisoners committed to their custody."[1] "Fees were payable for admission, for detention in this or that part of the prison, for a separate room or a share thereof, for a bed, for a mattress."[2] Fees were even exacted for putting on irons and for striking them off. If the prisoner had plenty of money he could hire a lodging in the governor's house and live as if he were in an hotel, sending out for food and wine, and visited by his friends. If he could not afford this standard he remained on "the Common Side", in a den of noise, squalor and stench. The only point in which some prisoners of today would think Newgate was superior to the modern prison was that during the daytime at least there was no segregation. At night the men and women on the Common Side were locked up separately, but during the day men and women, their families and friends, all congregated together, and it was the society of this Witches' Sabbath that ensured the young and innocent offender's coming out of gaol versed in all the knowledge of the hardened criminal.

The only sort of people to be reasonably comfortable in such surroundings were those like Jenny Diver, with plenty of money, thoroughly at home in the society of the place, no prey to fears, and prepared to turn the situation to advantage at the least opportunity. Jenny was "maintained handsomely" by the gang, this being one of the articles of their charter. She, at least, would lack nothing the place could supply, including the considerate and respectful treatment

---

[1] B. M. Jones, *Henry Fielding, Novelist and Magistrate*. [2] Ibid.

Jane Webb

the gaoler and his assistants naturally showed to a lady with so many guineas at command. The function of the gaol as a place of detention only is evinced in the most extraordinary manner by the fact that so much stolen property was allowed to be brought inside its walls. During her two months' detention in Newgate Jenny employed herself by turning "fence"; she bought, as Guthrie delicately says, "such things as came her way". She bought so much property that when it was all packed up it nearly filled a waggon. Meanwhile the gang were making frenzied efforts to prevent their inspired leader from being sent abroad. The *Weekly Miscellany* of April 21, 1738, said: "This Webb is reckoned one of the tip-top hands at picking of pockets and is well known at Newgate by the name of Mrs. Murphy. She belongs to a large gang of pick-pockets that attend the Play Houses, etc., who declare if it cost Two Hundred Pounds she shan't go abroad." The *London Post* of April 13 had also celebrated her: "She is one of the expertest hands in town at picking pockets; she used to attend, well dressed, at the Opera House, Play Houses, etc., and, it is reckoned, made as much annually by her practice as if she had the fingering of the public money."

The gang's efforts, however, were unavailing, and all they could do, since Jenny had to go, was to send her off in style. On June 7, 1738, she and thirty-seven convicts were put on board a lighter, to be carried down the Thames to Gravesend, where the galley *Forward* awaited them. The gang had packed up Jenny's clothes and the property that had come her way in Newgate and had it all sent on board in a cartload of trunks. Their grief at parting with her may have been mitigated by an idea that they would see her again before so very long.

On board, Jenny's natural distinction, her ready money and her trunks and packages in the hold, procured her, as usual, distinguished consideration. The captain did not treat her as he treated the rest of the passengers, and she was put on shore with her goods at the first port in Virginia the ship touched at. Again, one is amazed at the contrast between the savagery of the sentence inflicted by the state and the utter carelessness with which it was carried out. Jenny remained in America less than a year. "She stayed no longer than to see the country, for business in her way could not be transacted there." When she returned to England, however, she had to be especially cautious, since as an escaped convict her fate, if she were caught, would be the gallows. She did not immediately set up in London again, but made another of her "progresses" in country districts. She returned before long, however, to her favourite haunts, to London Bridge, the Royal Exchange, the Play Houses and St. Paul's.

A thief called Carter one day brought Jenny some articles, and as she paid him for them he told her that if she would lend him twenty guineas for a week he would be very glad to give her twenty-five guineas at the end. Jenny was on fire with curiosity to know what he could be doing that made it worth his while to pay such an enormous rate of interest. Carter asked, had she ever heard of a liquid that dissolved gold? and he showed her a crucible with a little lump of gold at the bottom. Jenny was wild with interest, but her native caution still prevailed and she would not lend him twenty guineas. Soon afterwards she heard that Carter was in the King's Bench prison and she went to visit him, sounding him in a roundabout way to know if he were prepared to part with his secret? Carter was evasive, he said he had now taken in a partner called David Roberts without whose permission he could not disclose anything; he also warned her that as an act had recently been passed making it a capital felony to diminish or debase the king's coinage, she should be exceedingly cautious how she tried her own hand at "sweating the guineas". Jenny saw he did not mean to tell her anything to the purpose, and having acquired

Jane Webb

the rudiments of the idea, she began to experiment for herself. She produced a liquid that withdrew a little gold from the coin, but she could not then separate the gold from the liquid. She tried to do this by boiling the liquid in a crucible, "but it all flew away". Jenny was exasperated and threw all her implements into a ditch in St. George's Fields, but soon afterwards she fell in with a chemist, who told her how to separate the gold from the liquid. She went home and tried again, but could not do it any better than before, and the guineas she had "sweated" were so much discoloured that she could not pass them, so all was a dead loss. She determined that Carter must be persuaded to part with the secret, but, for all her determination, she was on risky ground with him. Carter was not like her old associates, to whom she gave unstinted loyalty and from whom she received it again. Carter was out to make the most advantageous compromise he could, with whomsoever. One evening he accepted an invitation to supper at Jenny's lodging to discuss the business, and leaving on the pretext of going to fetch his tools, he came back with a band of officers to arrest her. Fortunately Jenny spied their approach from an upper window and made herself scarce just in time. Even this did not deter her in her determined pursuit of the magic secret; she approached Carter yet once more, and showing him a thirty-six shilling piece she had boiled till it was black, asked him if he could bring that to its colour again? Carter said he could and that he would let her into the whole process for twenty guineas. Jenny said ten, so "they disagreed and parted". Jenny now tried filing the gold coins, and by assiduous working she collected about ten pounds' worth of gold dust which she hid in a tobacco box under her bed, but somebody broke in and stole it. She suspected Carter. She pursued her experiments in "sweating" but still could not make it come right, until at last she found that in dealing with Carter she had been approaching the business from the wrong end. She now came into touch with his partner Roberts, and found, like the old woman in the fairy tale, that the dogs would bark and that she was herself after all. Roberts enlisted under Jenny's colours at her first approach. He showed her the whole process of sweating and went with her to a refiner's who would buy their produce. Under Roberts' tuition Jenny was able to sweat the guineas in such a manner that they would still be accepted, though they were each three shillings' worth "light". It was as well, none the less, to pass them as soon as possible, and whenever Roberts and Jenny went into shops they were sure to want change for a guinea. They worked so profitably and so fast that the number of guineas Jenny had ordinarily in hand was nothing like enough for them. They got into touch with a man called Rogers who kept a public house and collected gold for sweating. So much found its way to him that at last his doings attracted attention. His house was searched and in a box a hoard of three hundred new guineas was discovered, "which smelt so strong of the liquor they had been steeped in, as left no doubt of the game somebody had been at".

Jenny was now so much enamoured of this art that she thought of taking to it entirely, but she considered that it might be better to practise it abroad, and she turned over the idea of going to Lisbon, where there would be plenty of gold, she thought. These ideas were passing in her mind one morning as she looked into the Three Hats at Islington. In the coffee room two men were poring over a newspaper, and she asked them civilly if there were any news. Yes, they said, "the noted Jenny Diver was advertised for petty treason for diminishing the king's coin". Jenny was like the lightning that has disappeared before anyone can say that it was there. Her implements were destroyed, her clothes and belongings packed up and sent to Chatham and she, in man's dress, had bargained with a captain to take her over

Jane Webb

to Calais, before she paused to inform her friends of what had happened. She was to join the captain's boat at Ramsgate. When she got to Ramsgate, however, the wind blew so strong the captain would not put out. This gave Jenny leisure to write to some of the gang, and, having time on her hands, she could not resist the temptation of buying ingredients and making up some more of her liquor. In the meantime her associates had come down to Ramsgate and bargained with the captain to take them all across for twenty guineas. They were Carter, Roberts, his wife and his wife's brother. Alas, these were not the old brigade. Roberts only was thoroughly reliable. While the winds battled, the captain had been reading the newspapers, and he now came up to his ambiguous young passenger and told her he had "smoked" her disguise. He added that he had a pretty shrewd idea that she was wanted. Jenny said, if he would set out at once and no questions asked, he should have four or five guineas more, and from that moment until they were actually on board she never let the captain out of her sight.

Out at sea, it became apparent that Jenny's influence over her confederates was no longer potent, but that she still had formidable powers of her own. Half-way across the Channel a quarrel started, a thing that could never have occurred with the old gang who "knew each other's meanings by a nod" and acted in perfect unity with each other. The falling-out proved disastrous, for the captain joined it, "damned them all for rogues" and threatened to put back to Dover and deliver them up to justice. Roberts assumed command. He picked up a stave and swore he would knock the captain and his crew overboard if they did not go on, but now the weakness of the coalition made itself felt. Roberts's brother-in-law took the captain's part and urged him to take them all back, "but Jenny gave him a stroke and knocked him into the sea, which altered his tone, and it was with difficulty they got him into the boat again". This settled the captain's hash, and the rest of the voyage was performed uneventfully. Once on French soil, however, the flaw in their unity appeared again. The brother and sister were clearly anxious to dissociate themselves as soon as possible. Mrs. Roberts now ran to the Customs House and denounced the party. The Customs officers at once started to search the luggage and, sure enough, found in Jenny's a little box of tools and a bottle of acid; but their search gave Jenny a scant breathing space, enough for one so mercurial. She was away to Dunkirk. Whether she still wore man's attire, or carried enough money on her person to buy a set of French clothes is not revealed, but at Dunkirk she made an interesting acquaintance with Mr. Henry Justice, a gentleman who had been transported for stealing books from Cambridge University. Jenny was considering whether she might not set up there, exchanging French silver for the guineas brought over in the pockets of English travellers; but while she meditated taking Mr. Justice into her confidence, and letting him into the whole art of "sweating", he came to her himself, told her that he now knew who she was, and that it would be best for her to be off. Jenny took the hint and flitted away, making a wide détour through Flanders. When she returned to London, she remained hidden for six weeks in a house in Fountain Court; but seclusion was not only irksome, it was unprofitable. She made her way out, and, taking her tools with her, for she could not bring herself to relinquish this fascinating but perilous employment, she made a great circular tour of Basingstoke, Salisbury, Blandford and Gloucester. She came to rest at Bath. Here she hired a room and never worked except at night, so as to avoid suspicion.

Strangely enough, she still allowed Carter to be one of her associates. She heard that there was an inn to let at Coventry, and thinking it might prove a profitable business in itself and afford a hiding place for other activities Jenny went down there with Carter and a few companions. The present owner of the inn was a widow, Mrs. King, who was very favourably impressed by Carter's appearance. Jenny at once noticed this, and she told Carter he must make the most of it. Within three weeks the marriage had taken place, and now the gang had free board and lodging at the inn, but it turned out that the position was not as good as they had believed at first. When the news of Mrs. King's second marriage became known, every day brought some fresh creditor of her first husband's, and so much "mischief" was set abroach that the gang, including Carter, decided to cut the connection. Jenny, who had taken seventeen pounds "profit" during her stay, roamed away to Bristol, but at fourteen years old she had had "an itching desire to see London" and for the rest of her life the itch never left her for long. Always she came darting back to the city where her rewards were the greatest and her risks the keenest.

She now took a house in Marigold Court off the Strand. She went into business at once as a fence and she also set up a billiard-table, for resort in the daytime, and a hazard table for clients at night. The sort of company these attractions brought her was exactly that from which she made her best profits. She now made a very good income from these various lines of occupation and she fell in with a new set of companions. There was the brilliant Bob Ramsay, who had been a lawyer but was now a rogue. He had a vein of quickness and audacity something like Jenny's own, and his escapades, such as his posing as a doctor and attracting a large clientele in the city of Chester where he offered advice gratis for all distempers, Tuesdays and Wednesdays, for the men, Thursdays and Fridays for the women, an exploit which ended in his bewitching and robbing an heiress, show a power of sustained improvization and dramatic skill comparable with hers. There were Steevens and Young, both highwaymen, and most accomplished and desperate of all, there was young Harry Cook. Gordon said: "England has never produced a more fearless or daring robber than this man." Cook was but twenty-seven when he was hanged in 1741. He was thus about nine years younger than Jenny, but he may have been the father of her child, who was three years old at her own death in 1740. She had been known to visit a man in Newgate, who was said to be her husband, to bring him food, and also to dispense charities to other prisoners.

Whoever the father were, he would seem to have been one of the newer associates. We hear no more of the original gang, of the lover who acted as her footman with such skill and faithfulness, of the fence Johnson, or of Ann Murphy. Whether repentance or the gallows had claimed them, they had given place to a more erratic, less disciplined crew.

Cook did not take to the road through want, but rather from what the psychiatrists call "maladjustment". He was the son of respectable parents in Houndsditch and had been taught the leather-cutting trade which he practised in Stratford; but he quarrelled with his father, got deep into debt and resolved to turn highwayman. He bought his first pair of pistols off a stall in Moorfields and started to rob on the Essex Road and Finchley Common. He was caught before long and came up at the Old Bailey, but a stroke of extraordinary good luck procured his acquittal: his victim was unable to swear to his identity. The night following his acquittal he engaged in a great house-breaking expedition at Bow. This brought him acquainted with the highwayman Steevens, and a previous acquaintance of Cook's named Young, who had once kept an apothecary's shop in Stratford, introduced them both to Jenny.

Perhaps their brief stay in the inn at Coventry had put the idea of ale-house keeping into Jenny's head. At all events she became the proprietor of a little ale-house, rural and remote, on the side of Enfield Chase. She was now the fence

Jane Webb

of several highwaymen, and in this inn, which was run for her by "one Trotter", she "entertained her men and kept them close that none should see them". Once more her ascendancy reigned, her powers of organization and the faithful protection she extended to her less cautious and cool-witted subordinates. From the little inn in the tree-covered waste, at the side of the lonely road, the gang issued out by twos, threes and fours, towards distant London, and "robberies were committed even at noonday about town and the vicinity by this gang who increased in numbers and audacity to an alarming pitch".

Cook and Steevens worked together till the latter met an abrupt end. They were attempting a hold-up of the Colchester stage coach, and a Colonel Mawley who was riding behind in the basket shot Steevens dead. After this, Cook changed his beat and robbed in Kent and Surrey, but he was now notorious as a desperate highwayman. Never again could he hope that a victim who had once caught sight of him would fail to recognize him in the dock. He found himself "closely watched" on his new raids, so returned once more to his old haunt. In Stratford itself, he stood by while his companions robbed a gentleman called Cruikshank. The latter defended himself manfully and called out to Cook to help him. Cook stepped up and shot him, remarking that "dead men tell no tales". While the penalty for highway robbery was death, the victim stood little chance of getting away with his life. If the robber were caught, the murder made his own fate no worse, and the murder might give him a chance of escape.

This episode, however, made Cook "a little shy of appearing in public". Jenny was anxious not to lose the services of so expert a hand, and she decided that Cook should go into the country to recover his tone. She equipped him like a gentleman and he went off to try the air of Woburn in Bedfordshire. Here he married a woman with some money,

Six Criminal Women

but the marriage did not last long—no longer, perhaps than the money—and Cook took to the road again with a Captain Hall. They went into Hertfordshire and "recruited their pockets" from the coaches between Mimms and St. Albans.

What had happened meantime to Jenny's establishment in Marigold Court, to her rustic retreat on Enfield Chase? It was characteristic of such an existence as hers that nothing good lasted for very long, that her fortune bobbed up and down like flotsam in a strong tide; but while her vigour and vivacity remained at their youthful pitch, each fortunate phase as it receded was replaced by something new. But now nothing seemed open to her except pick-pocketing, at which, Guthrie says, she was still "a constant practitioner". By the time she was thirty-five, however, though she had gained a vast experience, she had lost a little of her dexterity; the polish of her performance was no longer quite what it had once been. Not only that, but she no longer was able to surround herself with assistants on whose absolute fidelity she could rely. The woman who was taken up for a somewhat bungling street robbery on January 17, 1740, was hardly the same creature as the girl of seventeen who was chosen as their leader by a gang of expert and hardened criminals, as the brilliant prestidigitator who could squeeze a man's hand and then withdraw her own with his ring in it.

On January 17, between six and seven in the evening, Jenny, wearing a red cloak and carrying a black hat under its folds, so that she might hastily alter her appearance by putting it on, was walking past the Mansion House with Mrs. Catherine Huggins, alias Elizabeth Davies and a male member of the gang whose name did not transpire. It is an interesting commentary on the state of the roads in eighteenth-century London that at the corner of the Mansion House the ground was so water-logged planks had been thrown down to make the way passable. A young woman called Mrs. Judith Gardener, with thirteen shillings and a

Jane Webb

halfpenny in her pocket, was coming down Sherbourne Lane, and as she approached the corner by the planks the man who accompanied Jenny went up to the young woman and seized her by the hand, saying: "I will help you over, child, for if you should slip into the water you would be worse off." Judith Gardener answered crossly that she did not want any help, but the man kept hold of her right hand, raising it above her head and squeezing it so tightly that her fingers were quite "numm'd". At that moment she felt Jenny's hand in her pocket. She pushed her left hand in and grasped Jenny's, which had already got hold of her two half-crowns and seven shillings.

"Hussy!" shouted Judith Gardener. "You have got my money!" Upon this, she said, Jenny struck her such a blow on the face that she was obliged to let go the pick-pocket's hand. The instant Judith Gardener raised her voice the male robber slung his hook and charged straight into the arms of a coal-merchant, Mr. Samuel How, who was passing by with his sister and her child. Mr. How at once collared the fugitive, whereupon Jenny and Elizabeth Davies both flew at him and scratched his face, shouting that the poor man he was molesting was "a good housekeeper who lived the other side of Moorfields". Mr. How, his energies diverted by this spirited attack, let go the robber, who at once took to his heels and was seen no more. Jenny had saved his life at the cost of her own. She deserved a better confederate. A green-grocer, Mr. Day, had been called out by the noise, and between them he and Mr. How hustled Jenny and her companion down Bearbinder Lane in search of an officer, without success, and then to Devonshire Square, hoping to find a magistrate, but with no more luck. They decided therefore to go straight to the Old Bailey. On the way there Jenny offered Mrs. Gardener a guinea and a gold ring "to put up the matter", but the offer was indignantly refused. At the Old Bailey the party found the Lord Mayor still sitting, though it was now eight o'clock on a Saturday night. A warrant was immediately made out and the two women were committed to Newgate, and brought up for trial the following Tuesday.

There had been but three days to prepare a defence, but the faithful members of the gang had done their best. The line decided upon was that the robbery of Mrs. Gardener had been committed by a man quite unknown to either Jenny or Elizabeth Davies and that the two women had not been in each other's company at the time but had each approached the scene in the company of other friends, who were there to testify to the fact as well as to give evidence to the eminently respectable and law-abiding characters of the accused.

Lydia Walker said that Jenny was her lodger: "I live in the Walk which leads from Holywell Mount to Hoxton and take in quilting. Mrs. Young I have known better than a year. She rents a room in my house at two shillings a week and takes in plain work . . . ! I never saw anything (of her) but what was modest and well-behaved." Amelia Harwood declared that she had been Jenny's sole companion on the fatal evening, "And a very good workwoman she is; she has worked for a great many good housekeepers that I know, and they liked her extraordinarily well. I met her," continued Mrs. Harwood, lying with great circumstance, "in Whitechapel, and desired her to go with me to Holborn Bridge, so just as we came by the china shop at the corner of the market there was a crowd; it was about six o'clock, and Mrs. Young said: Somebody is beating his wife, and she would go to see what was the matter. We went up a passage and the woman laid hold of her and said: You are one of the women that helped to rob me!" Ann Jones claimed that she and Mrs. Davies had been together the whole evening, that they had indeed passed by the scene of the crime, but that they never saw "that woman in the red

Jane Webb

cloak", pointing out Jenny with a fine show of ignorance, "all the way".

These alibis were supported by members of the gang, who all claimed to have been passing and to have seen and heard cries after a male thief. John Michena said he heard a woman cry out: "Lord have mercy on me, the rogue has picked my pocket!" but he could testify no further, for, he said, "I did not stop but went directly home." This may have been as well, for the witness whom the gang had put up to tell a complete story showed an utter lack of preparation and conviction. John Howard, a dresser of hats, asserted that he was going up Bearbinder Lane to a wine vault, to fetch away a hat to dress, and as he did so he heard shouts of "Stop *him*! Stop *him*!" and then to his surprise he saw two sober, well-conducted women arrested. Mr. Howard's evidence may have been good in itself, but he appeared to be speaking it by rote, and his manner was not lost on the jury. One of them asked him to whom the wine vault belonged? He did not know. Was it a wholesale or retail establishment? He could not say. Who was the gentleman whose hat he was to dress? He did not know his name. A counsel asked: "Is it usual to dress hats for people whose names you do not know?" Mr. Howard said it was quite usual. He would take the hat to the wine vault and the drawer would call out for the gentleman who was expecting it. The jury impatiently dismissed such shambling improvization. Jenny had indeed come down in the world. Such a bungler as this would never have had the entrée to the gang in the gay days of Bristol Fair.

The Sessions report of the trial gives only a part of the proceedings and altogether omits the judge's summing up, but despite its fragmentary nature it is extraordinarily vivid: there are the muddy streets and the tight, elegant little housefronts, the murky passages and courts, the lively jostling crowds, all growing dim under the twilight of a January evening at six o'clock. There is the august, classical pile of the Mansion House, its pillars and portico rising up into the dusk, and the morass before it where they had had to throw down planks. Over the planks comes carefully a young woman, who is marked by Jenny and her companions. There is a struggle and Jenny snatches from her pocket two half-crowns and seven shillings. "Guilty. Death." The abrupt termination, in large Gothic lettering, gives a shock to the reader, even after two hundred years, but it is a shock almost of incredulity. The pang to the prisoner, though mortal, had at least no surprise in it. She had hoped and may even have expected to escape it, but she had been familiar with it as a possibility every day for the past fifteen years.

It is a common accusation that we feel leniently towards crimes which do not affect ourselves and with intense bitterness towards those that do, but it is not only the safe distance of two centuries which makes one inclined to view Jenny more favourably than the spiv of today. Thieving is an odious social offence and no one will put forward Jenny Diver, attractive as she was, as anything but a criminal, who practised, though with style and artistry, a trade that was essentially sordid and base. But she might well have argued that the poor owed society no allegiance. The public callousness of the time is almost unbelievable. The Foundling Hospital had been started because to the humane Captain Coram it had seemed a cruel thing to see unwanted babies dying or dead at the roadside. If Jenny had failed to maintain herself and had had no friends to help her, she would have starved to death. The utter unconcern of society as a whole, apart from the charitable impulse of private people, towards the plight of the poor was revenged on them by the depredations of pick-pockets and cut-purses and highwaymen, every other one of whom was a potential murderer. Fielding would have heard Jenny condemned to hang without a qualm, but he argued forcibly, again and again, that

Jane Webb

you cannot put down crime until you have reduced the poverty that engenders it. No one would now deny this obvious truth, but when, as happens nowadays with increasing frequency, the law-abiding citizen is burgled, swindled or robbed with violence, it adds the last touch to his discouragement to remember that he and his family have been taxed to the bone to provide the criminal with the most elaborate social services.

Another difference in Jenny's favour between her and her modern counterpart, though admittedly it is one of less than moral importance, is her æsthetic superiority. The appalling vulgarity of the mass-production age has supervened since Jenny's day; her less successful contemporaries displayed rags, sores, lice and dirt to a degree utterly unknown even among the worst cases revealed by our own social surveys, but she herself, in an age of the most remarkable elegance, could pass unnoticed among elegant people. The tight plain bodice and sleeves, the hooped skirt, the flat round hat set straight on the head, the neckerchief and gloves, were a form of dress universally worn, in differing degrees of fineness. It is deeply instructive to compare this beautiful outline with the costume evolved by the modern female of Jenny's order: a pair of trousers, shoes with high heels, a belted overcoat, a head tied up in a scarf, long, dirty, painted, peeling nails and a perpetual cigarette. The modern absence of any popular æsthetic sense is never more fearfully apparent than when some slight imitation of the past is attempted. In recent years two styles of eighteenth-century hairdressing have been revived: that of Madame de Pompadour, and the Regency mode of carrying the ends of the hair to the top of the head. Both these coiffures were designed to complement long skirts, the great hoop of the 1750s and the limp, nymph-like gown of the 1800s. To see either of them on a female whose skirt ends at the knees, revealing a pair of bare and mottled legs, is to be reminded yet again of what happens to taste when it ceases to be dictated by the cultivated class. To compare the clothes of the women in Hogarth's pictures of the under-world with those of their modern counterparts is like comparing the shapely, spirited, racy sentences in which Mr. Guthrie describes his criminals with the jargon of the modern reporter.

It would show a lack of proportion, indeed of common sense, to regard Jenny as a heroine or even as a martyr. By the standards of the time she had deserved her fate many times over, and she had enjoyed an uncommonly good run for other people's money. One can but feel indignation that she should have met her death in saving a ruffianly coward, yet it was a good way to make an end, and perhaps the end itself was fortunate: for what alternative was before her? A reformation at the age of thirty-five, after twenty years of the excitements and quick rewards of thieving, was next door to impossible, and the older and less agile she became the lower she would have sunk, into miseries and horrors such as we are glad not to think about.

Whether she experienced any real repentance in her last days seems very doubtful. The only stilted and ineffective passage in Guthrie's account is the opening paragraph which is supposed to be in Jenny's own words, in which she proclaims her repentence and calls upon her friends to repent also. These frigid and unconvincing exclamations are soon brushed aside as Mr. Guthrie settles down to tell his story, in all the vigour and vivacity of a man writing, quite unknown to himself, in the greatest age of English prose. That Jenny's histrionic ability, united though it was with an underlying coolness of temper, caused her when thoroughly worked upon to shed the tears described seems probable enough. She seems to have shown some real concern for her little girl. This is the only child of whom there is any mention. (The subjects of Mercury are said to marry, or form a connection, early in life, but to have very small

Jane Webb

families.) She sent for the woman who had been the child's wet-nurse and told her she was not anxious about its livelihood—that was provided for (no doubt by the industry of its mother); but she wanted someone to visit it, and when it was old enough to give it good advice about leading an honest life. This the nurse promised to do.

Jenny's courage and coolness, with but one failure, remained with her to the last. Condemned criminals rode from the gaol to Tyburn with their coffins in the carts beside them and the rope that was to hang them round their necks. On the morning of March 18 the hangman came to the prisoners in the Press Yard, and as he approached Jenny to halter her she appeared "extremely shocked", but the moment passed, and she was able to make the figure at Tyburn that was due to herself. There were twenty condemned criminals on this occasion, and the rest of them went ahead, in seven carts, accompanied by Mr. Guthrie. The presence of the famous Jenny Diver had made the authorities apprehensive of what the crowd might do, and the special precautions taken against an attempt at rescue added very much to the stateliness of Jenny's last appearance. The seven carts were merely escorted each by two of the Light Horse; then, preceded by a file of musketeers and followed by eight of the Light Horse, with drawn swords, and forty infantry, came a mourning coach. In it rode Jenny, dressed all in black, a veil over her face, and attended by the Rev. Mr. Broughton. When she had gone for transportation, her trunks had filled a waggon and she had been treated quite differently from the other convicts, and the same air of distinction and privilege accompanied her to the gallows.

The prisoners were stood upon two carts under the gallows, and the last rites were paid. Guthrie, who was in charge of these proceedings, had a somewhat harassing task upon his hands. The prisoners were very earnest in following their prayers, which Guthrie was conducting according to the Church of England as by law established; but some of the condemned had been joined by clergymen of their own, whose private ministrations were causing a disturbance that Guthrie felt obliged to check. "On one side was a Papist praying loudly to the Saints, whom I was obliged to rebuke, by telling him he acted contrary to the laws of our land and might be complained on, upon which he became silent; on the other was a Methodist, who by his behaviour seemed rather crazy than devout, whom we also silenced and went on with our prayers."

The prisoners joined in the saying of the penitential psalm, then the horses, urged forward, pulled the carts rapidly away from beneath their feet, and their bodies dangled in the air.

There have been much worse criminals than Jenny who have met with a much milder fate. Although she was incorrigibly anti-social, she had some qualities that are rare even among the respectable. At fourteen she sent her young companion's possessions after him when she could have kept them, and it was the same spirit that made her throw away her life in going to the rescue of her worthless confederate, and, in spite of her own condemnation, urge so strongly her companion's innocence that Elizabeth Davies' sentence was mitigated to transportation. Decent and good-natured, cool, spritely and elegant, she was in many ways an admirable character. She would have been a charming companion, provided one had left one's money at home.

THE BALHAM MYSTERY

Some lives suggest irresistably the theory of reincarnation; actions which their possessors commit appear to us no worse or more momentous than the identical actions committed by scores of others with complete impunity, yet in these lives their consequences are so profound, so ruinous, it seems impossible to believe that the cruel punishment was earned by the single act. We feel that some awful pattern of cause and effect is being woven on a plane that is beyond our immediate vision: that the retribution has been set in motion by the single act, but that it was earned elsewhere and at another time; that what we see in front of us is a short length of a chain whose beginning and end are hidden from us in this existence.

Such feelings are hard to withstand when one thinks about the Balham Mystery, with its victim, its criminal who was never named and the broken lives left in its wake.

The Campbells were a wealthy merchant family, with a country house, Buscot Park, in Berkshire, and a town house in Lowndes Square. They had several children, of whom the most interesting was their daughter Florence. This was an unusually attractive girl, radiant and gentle, but with a somewhat erratic strain of self-will. She was of a small, pretty, rounded figure, with large and widely set blue eyes, and a mass of hair that is variously described as red-gold and bright chestnut. There was no difficulty in marrying off such a charming creature, and in 1864, when she was nineteen, she was married to Captain Ricardo, a wealthy young guards officer of twenty-three.

Six Criminal Women

Captain Ricardo undoubtedly had a great deal of money, but there his eligibility as a husband might be said to have begun and ended. The fact that he had married a beautiful girl of nineteen did not deter him from keeping a mistress, and the amount he drank seemed deplorable even to a hard-drinking age. Nor was he a man who could be left to drink himself under the table while a wife quietly pursued an independent existence; the unhappy bride was subjected to all the harassing torments of reconciliations, promises, relapses and promises again. Such an introduction to married life would have broken down most girls, and Florence was particularly unfitted to bear it. Her vitality was high—her glowing appearance and her strong natural faculty for enjoyment proclaimed it—but it was a purely physical characteristic. When she was subjected to any emotional strain she went to pieces, and the experiences of five years as Captain Ricardo's wife had all but reduced her to a nervous wreck. If she had been a plain woman, who had learned to adapt herself to slights and to make the best of what was going, she would have managed better; but she had come from an affectionate home, in all the natural self-confidence of a lovely girl. The shock and bewilderment, the undreamed-of humiliations of her position, had undermined her completely. There was only one consolation which she had found in her married life. It was drink. She had found out that the best way to endure Captain Ricardo's weakness was to share it.

By the time she was twenty-four she had sunk into absolute ill-health. Her mother persuaded her to come away to Malvern to try the hydropathic cure, and Captain Ricardo in one of his fits of reconciliation and promised amendment was to join her there. It was hoped, with singular optimism, that he, too, might find benefit from the water treatment.

Malvern had long been a spa, but it had developed with great rapidity as the Metropolis of the Water Cure, since

The Balham Mystery

1842, when Dr. Wilson and Dr. Gully had settled there and introduced their system which had become nationally famous. Though Wilson had introduced the idea of hydrotherapy, which he had picked up abroad from a Bavarian peasant named Preissnitz, Gully was so much the abler man of the two that he soon became the leading figure, and in a few years had made Malvern famous all over the British Isles. His system consisted in the application of water in every form: packing in wet sheets, sitz baths, douches, compresses, showers whether lateral or horizontal, spinal washings, foot baths, plunge baths and friction with dripping towels. His patients included Tennyson, Carlyle, Charles Reade, Bulwer Lytton, Bishop Wilberforce and "a host of the favourites of society". Though his success was sensational, there was no suspicion of quackery about him. He was a thoroughly trained medical man; and though his success was no doubt assisted by his great personal magnetism, the influence this gave him over his patients was a legitimate attribute of the eminent doctor. He was now sixty-two, not tall, but dignified and erect, with handsome, clear-cut features and an expression of warmth and candour.

Florence Ricardo had once been taken to Dr. Gully when she was a child of twelve, so that her present visit to Malvern was in a sense the renewal of an old acquaintance. That she succumbed at once to the influence of Dr. Gully's personality needs no explanation and hardly an excuse. She was ill because she was miserable and miserable because she was ill. Dr. Gully treated her with the profound sympathy and scientific understanding, the warm, impersonal kindness, which only a doctor can bestow. She had never known anything like it. Her experience of men had begun at nineteen when she found herself married to a husband who left the house to go to a mistress and drank himself silly when he stopped at home. Though she was headstrong she was not self-reliant; she would have leaned on a husband if she could.

Six Criminal Women

As it was, her husband was weaker than she, and his scandalous ill-treatment of her alternated with fits of grovelling repentance and self-abasement. Dr. Gully, who was authoritative, calm and kind, provided exactly the support that her unhappy state cried aloud for; above all, he was an exceptionally able physician, under whose care she got well again. It was no wonder that when her whole nature turned towards him with gratitude and admiration, her emotion overpassed the prescribed boundary and turned into romantic love. The fact that Dr. Gully was old enough to be her father was no hindrance to this. Her devastating experience of a young husband made her yearn for the lover who would be also a father.

Matters were in this somewhat equivocal state when fresh outbursts on Captain Ricardo's part decided the Campbells that their daughter should not be asked to continue this existence; the outcome of their decision was that Captain Ricardo consented to a deed of separation by which Florence was to live apart from him and to receive an allowance of one thousand two hundred pounds a year. This took place in 1870. The following year, Captain Ricardo, who had retired to Cologne with a mistress, died there suddenly, before he had revoked the will made on his marriage. Thus at twenty-five Florence was left a widow, with four thousand pounds a year in her own right.

Her family regarded the event as a release, and yet the position was far from reassuring. Up till now Florence had been first under her parents' control, and then under the nominal control of a husband. She had not caused anybody anxiety, except by her unhappiness and ill-health, but if she had, her father or her husband could have exerted considerable pressure on her by the mere fact that she had no means of support except what either of them chose to give her. Now it was very different. As a widow, she was completely her own mistress, with a large income entirely at her own

The Balham Mystery

disposal. There she was, in Malvern, and there was Dr. Gully.

Released from the monstrous bondage in which the first years of her adult life had been passed, her wilful, luxurious nature now asserted itself. To look at the likeness of her face, with its large, emotional eyes, its expression of mingled softness and intensity, is to feel that it is no unkind or unreasonable judgment that the motive force which brought together her and Dr. Gully came from her. Dr. Gully was a very busy man, in a large and exacting practice; not only had he been grounded in the high traditions of his profession, but if he had not been a man whose emotions were under his own control he would never have achieved his remarkable success. On the other hand, if a determined siege were to be laid to him, this of all others was the time of his life when it might be expected to succeed. He was nearing the end of his professional life. Though left to himself he would no doubt have continued in practice for some time longer, he was within sight of the time when he would have relinquished it in any case. He was extremely well-to-do (the income from his practice was estimated at ten thousand pounds), and though he was in fact a married man, his son was grown up and his wife, who was in an asylum, had been separated from him for thirty years. If anyone could be excused for regarding himself as a free agent when in actual fact he was not it was surely a man in the position of Dr. Gully. On the other side, Florence was very young, but she was not inexperienced. However impetuous her approaches had been, he would have been very unlikely to admit them had she been an unmarried girl, but her misfortunes had made her a woman of the world, and she was responsible to nobody but herself. At the same time, she was not only fascinating but she had the charm of youth, and to Dr. Gully as a man of over sixty her devotion was not only enchanting, it was flattering to an unusual degree. It was difficult to prove at what date they became lovers, but it was afterwards considered certain that it was while Dr. Gully was still in practice at Malvern. A great deal depended on this point, and when it was regarded as having been proved the decision was fatally unfortunate for him.

Florence very early in her widowhood became at variance with her family, who strongly disapproved of her infatuation for Dr. Gully, and before long her parents told her that they would have no communication with her until she gave it up. So strong was the convention of the time that Mr. and Mrs. Campbell took this drastic step of refusing all intercourse with their daughter, although they imagined her infatuation to be indiscreet rather than actually immoral. It was a strange characteristic in a charming young woman that she was almost friendless. Perhaps her capacity to absorb herself in an emotional adventure argued a certain self-centredness that would repel a friend as it would attract a lover. At all events, her separation from her family left her without a social circle, and she accepted the offer of accommodation from her solicitor, Mr. Brooks, in his house on Tooting Common. Mr. Brooks had three daughters, for whom he employed a daily governess, an unremarkable woman of middle age, a widow named Jane Cannon Cox. The most noticeable feature of Mrs. Cox's appearance was her spectacles, which apparently had the effect of quite obscuring the expression of her face. Drawings of her emphasize this so much that it seems likely the glasses were tinted. Her dark hair, in one of the less prepossessing fashions of the time, was scraped back from her temples and so arranged that the top of her head looked pointed like a bee-hive. The dress of the 'seventies, which concentrated all the fullness of the drapery at the back, left the front of the figure, rigidly corseted, tightly outlined from the shoulder to the knee. The effect on Mrs. Cox's somewhat low and meagre frame was to give her the outline of a black beetle.

The Balham Mystery

Mrs. Cox had the efficiency and self-possession of a woman who has had to make her way against odds. Her husband had been an engineer in Jamaica, but he had died and left her to provide for three young sons. She had been assisted by a wealthy friend, a Mr. Joseph Bravo. By his advice she had invested her small amount of money in a furnished house in Lancaster Road, Notting Hill, which she let, while she herself went out as a governess to Mr. Brooks's family. Her three boys were placed at a school in Streatham for the sons of distressed gentlefolk. Quietness, respectability, usefulness and pleasantness to an employer were not, in Mrs. Cox's case, mere unselfconscious traits of character; they would more properly be described as weapons, held in an unfaltering grasp, with which she waged the battle with the world that was to win the livelihood of her children and herself. She was not in any sense attractive, but her powers of mind were considerable, and since these were all directed towards making herself agreeable to people more fortunately placed than herself it was not surprising that she was successful. She soon made herself pleasant to the rich, voluptuous young widow, then useful and at last indispensable. Dr. Gully meanwhile, in 1872, sold his practice and retired from Malvern. His retirement was a civic event; demonstrations of respect and gratitude were made by every class of society and the town acknowledged that it was his working there for thirty years which had brought prosperity to it. He did not immediately settle upon a house. He took lodgings opposite to Mr. Brooks's house on Tooting Common.

That Florence had no friends of her own did not mean that she felt able to do without them. Her infatuation for Dr. Gully was the most important thing in her life, but their liaison could not supply the want of a social circle. The usage of the time obliged the lovers to behave with the utmost secrecy and discretion. They could enjoy very little of each other's society in an open manner. Florence still needed a friend for daily wear, and as a rich and somewhat self-indulgent young woman she also wanted somebody to take the troubles of her establishment off her hands. It was not long before the idea of Mrs. Cox presented itself to her, irresistibly. Mrs. Cox seemed to have every qualification that Florence could imagine as desirable. She was excellent in household management, and she knew how to order an establishment for rich people, how to control a large staff of servants and to see that a high standard of comfort and elegance was maintained. Nothing was irksome to her, no trouble was too great; in a quiet and unobtrusive way she whole-heartedly identified herself with the owner of the establishment. Then, too, she was a gentlewoman; and though personally unattractive and in narrow circumstances, she was presentable as a companion, and in her tact, sympathy, affection and common sense she was quite invaluable. Mrs. Cox, on her part, was exceedingly happy to exchange the drudgery and poor pay of a governess for the luxury and freedom, the authority, of friend and companion to such an employer as Florence Ricardo. The opportunity was indeed exceptionally fortunate. The generosity of Florence's nature had had few outlets, and she thoroughly enjoyed being good to Mrs. Cox. Their footing was one of complete social equality; they called each other Florence and Janie. And Florence not only did everything possible to make her companion happy under her roof—Mrs. Cox received a salary of one hundred pounds a year, but her incidental expenses, which were all paid for her, including many items of her dress, came to three times this amount—but her employer took a warm interest in Mrs. Cox's three boys. Their school holidays were spent with their mother in Mrs. Ricardo's house.

When Florence left Mr. Brooks's house, taking Mrs. Cox with her, she settled herself for the time being in a house in Leigham Court Road, Streatham Hill. The house she

The Balham Mystery

had occupied in Malvern, where the great bliss of her life had come to her, had been called Stokefield, and she named this house Stokefield also. At her suggestion Dr. Gully bought a house which was available on the opposite side of the road. That a woman so astute as Mrs. Cox should not have realized on what terms her employer and Dr. Gully were anyone may believe who likes; but at least the polite fiction was kept up that the relationship was merely one of devoted friendship. Dr. Gully often came to meals. He called his hostess by her Christian name, and they kissed each other. In Mrs. Cox's opinion, he was "a very fascinating man, likely to be of great interest to women". She went so far as to say that, though she believed the friendship to be quite innocent, had Dr. Gully been unmarried it would no doubt "have been a match".

In this year, 1872, Dr. Gully and Mrs. Ricardo went for a holiday to the baths at Kissingen. They attempted no deceit; they travelled under their own names and occupied separate rooms in their hotels, but as a result of their time abroad Florence had a miscarriage when she came home. Dr. Gully attended her, but she was nursed by Mrs. Cox. She said that she had at the time entirely concealed from Mrs. Cox the cause of the illness, and made out, what she had in fact at first thought to be the case, that it was the result of a severe internal derangement brought on by the baths at Kissingen. Mrs. Cox's untiring devotion to her during weeks of illness and prostration established the companion's claim on her more firmly than ever.

In 1874 Florence decided upon a permanent house. This was an estate of ten acres known as the Priory at Balham. The house had been built in the early 1800s and was a charming example of the Walpole Gothic, simple, airy, graceful, that was later to be submerged in the hideous Municipal Gothic of the Victorian age. The Priory, with its pale tint, its crenellated roof, its arched doorway, and windows with pointed upper panes, belonged to the last era in English social life that produced charming architecture. On the front lawn stood a giant oak tree, said to be a hundred and fifty years old. Behind was the sunny "garden front", laid out in turf, gravelled paths and numerous flower-beds. There were a greenhouse, a grapehouse, a melon pit, large strawberry beds and a vegetable garden. Florence filled the house with luxury, gaiety and comfort. Her morning-room housed a sparkling collection of Venetian glass and opened into a small conservatory. She liked this effect so much that she repeated it in the drawing-room, where she threw out one of the windows to make a fernery. Here she assembled a grove of exquisite ferns, for some of which she had paid twenty guineas each. Horticulture was one of her keenest enjoyments and she kept the garden in a high state of perfection, filling the beds with flowers and planting standard rose trees everywhere. The Victorian age was one of hot summers, and the windows of the Priory were shaded with striped awnings, which added their inimitable touch of festivity to the scene of a well-kept English garden on a hot summer day. Another of Florence's pleasures was driving. She kept one carriage horse for her landau—this was driven by her coachman; but she drove herself in a phaeton with two "handsome actioned" cobs, called Victor and Cremorne. The pamphlet, *The Balham Mystery,* issued in seven numbers in 1876, contains instead of press photographs a series of pen-and-ink drawings of remarkable vividness. The press photographer has superseded the press artist, and it comes as a surprise to our generation to see how excellent the latter was. One of the illustrations shows Florence driving her cobs. The tiger sits behind with folded arms while she bowls along at a smart pace. The drawing shows a woman who drove very well. She wears a close-fitting jacket with a bow under her chin, and a wide-brimmed hat shaded by a feather, under which her hair streams away

The Balham Mystery

behind her ears. By her side, upright, collected and demure, sits Mrs. Cox.

Within a few months of Florence's having bought the Priory Dr. Gully bought a house in Bedford Hill Road, a few minutes away from the Priory lodge. The long slope of grass and trees terminating in the level ground of the Priory was unbuilt on, except for six houses, all of the same design, halfway up on the left-hand side. Dr. Gully took the first, which was called Orwell Lodge. He, like Florence, seemed to regard his new establishment as a permanent one. He furnished it from top to bottom and installed his own servants, of whom the chief was his butler Pritchard, who was devoted to him and had been with him for twenty years. The neighbourhood in 1875 was still extremely retired. Bedford Hill Road was so quiet that when Florence built a second lodge to open the estate on that side, though the new lodge stood directly upon the road without the protection even of a paling, the climbing roses she trained all over its front hung undisturbed. There were no censorious neighbours to overlook their private lives. Dr. Gully had a key to one of the doors of the Priory. The parlour-maid said: "I never opened the door to him, but I have found him in the house." He came frequently to lunch and stayed to dine. Once or twice when Mrs. Cox was away he stayed the night. The Priory coachman, Griffiths, had previously been in Dr. Gully's service. Now that Dr. Gully had left off practice, he did not keep a carriage and Florence had taken Griffiths on. He and his wife lived in the new lodge. Three or four times a week Griffiths drove the doctor and Mrs. Ricardo out in the landau. He would take up Dr. Gully in one of the quiet roads near his house, and set him down again before he reached the gate of Orwell Lodge. Sometimes they drove in to London, but more often their drives were through the undisturbed country about Tooting Common. On frequent occasions Florence, accompanied by her chaperone, would come to meals at the doctor's house. When this happened, the butler Pritchard could see that, though his master and Mrs. Ricardo were still very much attached to each other, the affair had become worn down to the level of ordinary existence. "They often quarrelled," he said.

The Bravos who had befriended Mrs. Cox lived in a large house on Palace Green, Kensington. The family of three were Mr. and Mrs. Bravo and the latter's son by a previous marriage. Charles Bravo, who had taken his stepfather's name, was the idol, not only of his mother, but of his stepfather also. He was a good-looking young man, with dark hair, rounded features and an expression at once pugnacious and egotistical. Mr. Joseph Bravo had brought him up from a child, educated him and seen him established at the bar. He doted on what he took to be the young man's great cleverness, and he loved him as fondly as if Charles had been in fact his son. Charles Bravo would not appear to have been strikingly gifted in the profession he had chosen. He was nearly thirty and his gains as a barrister were still almost nominal; but despite the fact that his stepfather gave him as much money as he could want, and that he had therefore no financial incentive to work very hard at an unrewarding profession, he did none the less devote himself to it. He went to his chambers every day and followed his profession as if his bread had depended on it. He had kept a mistress for the past four years, but the intense possessiveness of his mother and the indulgent kindness of his stepfather had so far prevented him from any inclination to be married.

One day Florence Ricardo went in the carriage to London to do a day's shopping and arranged to drop Mrs. Cox at Palace Green to call upon her friends, and to pick her up again on the way home. When, later in the day, Mrs. Ricardo's carriage was announced at the Bravos' door, Mrs.

The Balham Mystery

Bravo courteously sent out a request that Mrs. Ricardo would come in for a few minutes. It so happened that Charles Bravo was in his mother's drawing-room when the lady with bright auburn hair was shown in, but neither he nor she seemed at that time to take much notice of each other. The visit was short and, though extremely civil, was a purely formal one.

In 1875 Dr. Gully went abroad with some of his own relations. Though she might quarrel with him, Florence found her house dull and wearisome when he was not at hand, and to relieve the tedium of her lover's absence she took Mrs. Cox on a visit to Brighton. It was autumn, and Brighton was not gay. The beauty of the Regency squares and terraces was not appreciated by the taste of the 1870s, and the half-empty streets and the sea under autumnal mists and gales did not restore Florence's spirits. They had themselves photographed, but there was really very little to do.

Brighton, however, is within very easy distance of London and its advantage as a resort is that so many people run down from London for the day. By a really remarkable coincidence, in one of their walks they met Charles Bravo. The first meeting between him and Florence had passed off apparently in complete indifference on both sides, but on the second one it seemed as if a seed, long germinating, had suddenly burst into flower. Mrs. Cox was of course polite and cordial. It was not open to her to be anything else. Her paramount duty to herself and her children was to be pleasant to her employer, and whatever her opinion of the rapidly-forming intimacy might have been it would have had no weight with Florence. The latter might be dependent on her friend up to a certain point, but in anything which concerned her pleasures she was entirely her own mistress and intended to remain so.

Florence had not an admirable character, but one of her strongest charms was naturalness, and though her actions might be unwise or even discreditable they were always understandable and such as would arouse sympathy. Her passion for Dr. Gully was almost inevitable and the same might be said of its termination. She needed the love and protection of an elderly man to restore her after the shattering experiences of her first marriage, but when this influence had done its work and her being had recovered its normal balance she was ready to fall in love again with a man of her own age. Charles Bravo and she were both nearly thirty. She was independent by legal settlements and he was virtually so through the affection of his stepfather. If they chose to marry there would be no need of a long engagement. Charles Bravo was undoubtedly much attracted by Florence, but it is equally certain that what induced him to think of marrying her was her income. They were, however, well suited personally: young, vigorous, pleasure-loving, a virile man and an extremely feminine woman. The growth of mutual attraction went on fast and it was obvious that Charles Bravo's proposal would soon be made.

In October Dr. Gully returned to England and he came down to see Florence at Brighton. She now acted with great duplicity. She told Dr. Gully that the estrangement from her family, which could never be ended as long as her liaison with him lasted, had made her very unhappy for some time, and as her mother was now ill she wished earnestly to be reunited to her parents. She had decided therefore that the time had come for them to part. Dr. Gully behaved with the unselfish kindness of real affection, in spite of having received a very disagreeable shock. He had had no preparation for this event. He said afterwards: "I was very much attached to her at the time, and I had thought that she was fondly attached to me." But he said that she must do whatever she felt was necessary to her own happiness and wellbeing. In November Charles Bravo proposed to her and she accepted him. When Dr. Gully heard of this, he was at

The Balham Mystery

first thoroughly angry. After giving up his practice and his public position as one of the most eminent doctors of the day, and being at her beck and call for five years, he now found himself cavalierly thrown over for another man and shamelessly deceived as well. He wrote her one angry letter, but after that his anger subsided. He was sixty-six; and though the love affair had been an enchanting embellishment to his existence, what he really wanted now was peace and quiet, and a connection with a spoilt and exacting young woman, particularly one who was inclined to drink too much, was probably, as Sir John Hall[1] suggests, something that on calmer reflection he was quite prepared to give up.

In the rest of Florence's small circle feeling was much mixed. Her own parents were delighted, first that she should have put an end to the liaison for which they had felt obliged to disown her, and secondly that she was going to marry a man of suitable age, steady character and the prospect of great wealth. Their reconciliation with their daughter was complete. On the other side, however, the idea was received with open animosity. Mr. Bravo's feelings were not disclosed, but Mrs. Bravo, who would have been unwilling to see her son marry anybody, was horrified that he should marry Florence, whose independence, worldliness and sensual attractions filled her with hostile dismay. She would have stopped the marriage if she could, and once it was an accomplished fact she did the little that was in her power to upset its smoothness.

Mrs. Bravo's enmity to the match was open enough, but there was some elsewhere that expressed itself in a more subtle and tortuous manner. Florence had not been candid with Dr. Gully, but it was to the credit of her good feeling and also her common sense that she was perfectly open with Charles Bravo about her past. She told him the whole story

[1] *The Bravo Mystery and Other Cases.*

of her affair with Dr. Gully and he in return told her of his having had a mistress for the past four years, and each agreed that now all had been admitted they would never speak of the past again. Charles Bravo even discussed the matter with his future wife's companion. He said he should imagine that a woman who had once gone wrong would be even more likely to go straight in the future than one who had never strayed. What, he asked, was Mrs. Cox's opinion? Mrs. Cox had no doubt that he was quite right; but she did not stop there. She so much approved of the frankness the parties had shown to each other, that she wanted to see it carried even further. She suggested that the whole story of Dr. Gully's relation with her future daughter-in-law should be explained to Mrs. Bravo.[1] Charles flatly refused to consider any such idea. His mother was so much against the marriage already that to tell her such a thing as that was absolutely out of the question. It was, in any case, a private matter between his wife and himself and no concern of anybody else, even of his mother's. Still Mrs. Cox was urging her opinion to the contrary. It would be so much better, she thought, to have everything open and above-board. She was obliged, however, to give up the point. Charles Bravo, brusque, determined and short-tempered, was not amenable to unwelcome suggestions, especially from a paid companion.

The wedding was fixed for December 7, and meantime the settlements were being prepared. The Married Woman's Property Acts were not yet in operation and therefore everything in Florence's possession would become her husband's unless it were previously secured to her by settlement. Charles Bravo made a disagreeable impression on her solicitors because when he came to discuss the settlements and one of the firm offered him congratulations on the approaching marriage, he exclaimed: "Damn your congratulations!

[1] It is only fair to say that Florence's mother made the same suggestion.

The Balham Mystery

I have come about the money." His overbearing nature showed itself again on the question of the settlement itself. Florence's solicitor had wanted to secure to her, besides the income from her first husband's fortune, the Priory and all its furniture and movables. Charles Bravo acquiesced in her keeping the four thousand pounds a year in her own hands, but he demanded that the house and furniture should be taken out of the settlement and therefore become his. Florence took a keen delight in her charming estate and all her pretty furniture, her horses and carriage, and her jewellery, and in love though she was, a streak of her wilfulness showed itself. She refused to have these things removed from the settlement. The violence of Charles Bravo's temper now showed itself. He swore that rather than submit to sitting on a dining-room chair that was not "his own" he would break off the marriage, and she might take it or leave it.

Florence was in a quandary, and she did what she had done for the last five years, what was now second nature to her. She consulted Dr. Gully. They met in the Griffiths' lodge, and she told him her perplexity and asked his advice. She had already written to say that they must never see each other's face again, and Dr. Gully had accepted this decision as perfectly proper in the circumstances; but now that he had been sent for, he did not refuse to come. He behaved with the utmost kindness and sense. He said it was natural that Bravo should feel as he did, and the matter was not worth upsetting the marriage over. He advised her to give way. Then he wished her every happiness, kissed her hand and said good-bye.

Though it was Florence herself who had stated dramatically that they must never meet again, she did not seem entirely prepared to carry out her own edict. Dr. Gully, however, was prepared to do it for her. He saw that no other course was possible to a gentleman and a man of sense.

He sent back the key he had made use of by Griffiths to Mrs. Cox, and he told Pritchard that in no circumstances were Mrs. Bravo or Mrs. Cox ever to be admitted to Orwell Lodge. Pritchard was pleased enough to receive such orders; he said, "I had had quite enough trouble before when we had to do with them. I did not want my master bothered any more with them."

Florence was married on December 7, 1875, from her parents' house in Lowndes Square. It was a pleasant occasion, a marriage of affection between a good-looking young pair, with family approval and excellent prospects. The bridegroom's mother, however, had not brought herself to be present at the ceremony. She would only say that she hoped she might, in time, be able to feel more charitably towards her daughter-in-law.

Notwithstanding this piece of bad behaviour from old Mrs. Bravo, life at the Priory appeared to begin very happily; but there were indications, even in a month's time, that causes of disquiet existed, and that they showed themselves unusually soon. There was no doubt that husband and wife were strongly attracted to each other, but their happiness was made by their mutual passion, and it was sometimes threatened by the conditions of their daily existence. Charles Bravo had the power of arousing strong affection, but he was violent, and egotistical to the point of arrogance. On his marriage, twenty thousand pounds had been settled on him by his stepfather, and Mr. Bravo had afterwards given him another present of one thousand two hundred pounds; but apart from the stable expenses of the Priory, which he paid himself, all the expenses of the establishment, of any kind whatever, were paid out of his wife's income, while he had seen to it that all the property of the house was his. Florence spent freely, but she had always lived within her means; now, however, her husband began to domineer over her expenditure. Charles Bravo had certainly not been de-

The Balham Mystery

moralized by the prospect of inherited wealth; not only did he work hard, but he was what his friends called careful, and those who disliked him mean. To a man of this temper a wife who would spend twenty guineas on a fern was a subject of considerable disquiet. Using his legal powers as a husband and his influence as a newly married bridegroom, he began to consider where retrenchments might be made. As he visited his mother in Palace Green almost daily, he had plenty of opportunity to discuss his ménage with her, and old Mrs. Bravo was at no loss to suggest ways in which her daughter-in-law's pleasures might be curtailed. Florence had always kept a personal maid, but Charles, primed by his mother, persuaded her that she could do without one and manage with the help of the head housemaid. The fact that this housemaid, Mary Ann Keeber, was an exceptionally nice and sensible girl, perhaps made Florence acquiesce in the arrangement more easily than she might otherwise have done. The Priory gardens required the services of three gardeners; this, old Mrs. Bravo thought, and Charles agreed, was excessive, and he discussed with Florence a scheme for letting some of the beds go under grass. She was reluctant to give up one of her favourite pastimes, but to please her husband she was willing to entertain the idea. On her marriage the landau had been replaced by a carriage, for which two horses were jobbed. With Victor and Cremorne, this meant a stable of four. "What does one couple want with four horses?" exclaimed Charles. His mother agreed with him; Florence's cobs, she thought, were a quite unwarrantable expense. Florence was much annoyed at this final piece of interference, the more so because she knew who was behind it. She would not agree to parting with the cobs, and Charles Bravo relinquished the idea for the time being. His mind, however, was still earnestly bent upon saving his wife's money, and it occurred to him that with a husband, a butler, a footman, six women servants, three gardeners, a coachman and a groom, she really did not need the services of a companion. He began to look into the financial aspect of Mrs. Cox's employment. One day at his chambers, as he sat with his pen in his hand, calculating, he said to the barrister beside him that with salary, board and incidental expenses Mrs. Cox was costing them four hundred pounds a year. "Why," exclaimed his friend, "you could keep another pair of horses for that!"

Charles Bravo had no personal objection to Mrs. Cox. She lived as a member of his family and called him by his Christian name, and he spoke highly to his stepfather of her usefulness and her devotion to Florence; but the matter of four hundred pounds a year weighed on his mind considerably. Old Mr. Bravo knew that Mrs. Cox had an aunt in Jamaica from whom she had some modest expectations, and he advised her to go back to Jamaica with her boys. Mrs. Cox did not enlarge upon the topic; she merely said that she was not going.

She could of course decide whether or not she would go to Jamaica, but it would not be open to her to remain at the Priory once Charles Bravo had made up his mind to get rid of her. Florence was wilful and self-centred, but beneath her bright, petulant manner there was a pronounced weakness and dependence; she could be overpersuaded by affection and though emotional she had very little stamina. It would be only a matter of time before the cobs were laid down, and any other retrenchment Charles had in view would inevitably come about sooner or later. He had a passion for his wife and considerable affection for her when everything was going as he liked, but his method of achieving domestic tranquillity was by crushing all opposition.

Yet the recipe for a happy marriage cannot be defined like the recipe for a good pudding. Though Charles Bravo sounds as if he were in some ways almost as odious as Captain Ricardo, he and Florence were happy. Their domestic

The Balham Mystery

servants who saw them at all hours, and especially Mary Ann Keeber, who was often in their bedroom, all said that the pair were on the most affectionate and happy terms. His wife was not even disturbed by his occasional violence. Once he struck her, but the next moment his passion had subsided. "It was like a child's anger," she said.

Unknown to the servants, however, unknown to anybody except themselves and Mrs. Cox, there was, it is believed, one cause of very serious discord between husband and wife. That it existed is almost certain, but how acute it had become or what degree of importance was attached to it was never found out, and for more than seventy years the matter has aroused speculation and bewilderment. Florence Bravo asserted, and her statement was supported and amplified by Mrs. Cox, that after the marriage Charles Bravo developed a violent, retrospective jealousy of Dr. Gully. Though Mrs. Cox's statements are highly suspect, the wife's story, even though supported by no more trustworthy witness than Mrs. Cox, deserves at least a hearing. In their mutual confessions before the marriage she and Charles Bravo had agreed to overlook the other's past. It was common enough for a man to have had pre-marital entanglements, but in overlooking one on the part of his future wife Charles Bravo did what few men of the time would have been prepared to do. But just as he was not a sensitive man, so, too, he was not imaginative, and it was not until he himself was in possession of the woman he loved that the full realization of her having been Dr. Gully's mistress was brought home to him. The torment of sexual jealousy grew side by side with the delight of sexual love. Florence said that in spite of his promise he frequently upbraided her with her past love, that he cursed Dr. Gully as "a wretch" and said he would like to annihilate him. Meantime, so strictly did Dr. Gully keep to his seclusion that Charles Bravo had never once set eyes on him.

Six Criminal Women

In spite of her brilliant colouring, Florence was not robust. In January, the month after the wedding, she had a miscarriage, and in February 1876 she went to Brighton to recover. While she was there her husband wrote to her every day; the letters were afterwards read at a legal inquiry, and they were put in as showing nothing but the feeling of an anxious, devoted young husband who missed his wife. But one of them, Florence maintained, referred to their cause of distress. It was dated February 15 and written from Palace Green. It said: "I hold you to be the best of wives. We have had bitter troubles, but I trust every day to come the sweet peace of our lives will not so much as be disturbed by memories like those. . . . I wish I could sleep away my life till you return." It was suggested that the bitter troubles and the memories of them were those of the miscarriage. Florence declared that they were the raking up of burning grievance over Dr. Gully.

Neither Charles nor Florence Bravo had seen a sign of Dr. Gully since November of the previous year, but Mrs. Cox had seen him more than once. She fairly frequently made the short journey to town, on business about her house in Lancaster Road or to see her boys at St. Ann's School. On one occasion she met Dr. Gully in Victoria Street outside the Army and Navy Stores and he spoke civilly, and asked her to send him a book of press cuttings which he had once lent Florence and which had never been returned. Another time she met him on Balham Station. Dr. Gully had a cure for what was known as Jamaica fever, and Mrs. Cox asked him to let her have the prescription. He promised to do so, and a few days later it came to her by post addressed to the Priory. It was Charles Bravo's habit to meet the postman, take his wife's letters and open them before he gave them to her. On this occasion, Mrs. Cox declared, he met her with the letter in his hand and asked her if he might open it as it was addressed in Dr. Gully's hand. Mrs. Cox

The Balham Mystery

providently added that she had no idea how he had been able to recognize Dr. Gully's writing. She resented the request, she said, but she opened the envelope before his eyes and showed him that it contained nothing but the prescription. In the extraordinary maze to which the clue has never been found, incidents like this, with their double-edged aspect, add to the confusion like mirrors which are placed so to reflect turnings that the eye is lost between the reflection and the reality. Was this statement true? Grave doubts are cast upon it by the fact (of which Mrs. Cox's parenthesis looks like a clumsy attempt at covering-up) that it was scarcely possible that Charles Bravo should have been able to recognize Dr. Gully's handwriting. If it were not true, then it was obviously designed as an alibi for another incident, and if the second incident were not accounted for by the first's being true, then a new vista of murky possibilities is opened.

Florence returned from Brighton in recovered health, but shortly afterwards, on April 6, she miscarried again. The second miscarriage was more serious. She suffered much pain, weakness and sleeplessness. She stayed in bed for ten days, and her husband moved out of their bedroom and went to a spare room on the same landing, on the other side of an adjoining dressing-room. Mrs. Cox, whose own bedroom was on the floor above, came down and shared Florence's bed. During these ten days she met Dr. Gully again, on his way to Bayswater to stay with his son and daughter-in-law. Mrs. Cox told him how ill Florence was, of her pain, her backache and her sleeplessness and asked him what he would advise. The discreet reply on Dr. Gully's part would no doubt have been that Mrs. Cox should consult another doctor, but it was scarcely to be expected that Dr. Gully would make it. He recommended spinal washings and cold sitz baths, and knowing from his experience of her that Florence was "driven frantic by ordinary opiates" he said he would try to think of some sedative that might suit her and would send it to the Priory. Mrs. Cox hurriedly interposed, and giving as her reason the vigilance which Charles Bravo exercised over the post, asked Dr. Gully to send his prescription instead to her own house in Lancaster Road, where she would call for it. Dr. Gully did so. He left a half ounce green bottle, with a stopper covered in white kid, to be called for by Mrs. Cox. It contained laurel water. He had chosen it as something mild and incapable of producing disagreeable results.

Good Friday that year came on April 14. The weather was lovely, and Florence was getting up in the middle of the day. Over the holiday, Charles Bravo did not go up to his chambers; he stayed in the Priory, and Florence wrote a letter to his mother—so binding was the family etiquette of the time—in pleasant, domestic vein, saying, "Charlie is walking about the garden with a book under his arm, as happy as a king." He was in good spirits at the holiday, the fine weather and at his wife's recovering. Yet there was a slight upset after lunch. Florence had gone to her room to lie down, and her husband followed her, wanting to talk and be amused. She was weak and irritable and wanted him to go away and leave her to her rest. At last she absolutely ordered him out of the room. He was angry, and Mrs. Cox followed, attempting to soothe him. It was her own version of the affair that he shouted: "She's a selfish pig," and then said: "Let her go back to Gully." According to her, he was still angry that evening, and threatened to leave the house. By her own account, she went to his bedroom door and spoke to him in a placating manner. He replied, she said, by saying that he had no quarrel with *her*. "You are a good little woman," he said, and kissed her cheek.

As the weather was very fine, the Easter moon at its full must have filled the sky with light. In the tranquillity and

The Balham Mystery

silence of that quiet scene no sound from the outside world disturbed the sleeping Priory. On the garden side gravel paths glistened and conservatory panes glittered. In front, against the pale stuccoed façade, the giant oak tree stretched its arms, its black shadow thrown across the grass. The servants were all asleep in their quarters, the master was shut away in his single room. In the large bedroom at the head of the stairs Florence was in her bed, and beside her was Mrs. Cox. In the moonlight and the silence, what was said? It is as if the box containing the secret were in full view but the key is irretrievable.

On Easter Saturday the weather continued brilliantly fine and Florence and Mrs. Cox drove in the carriage to Streatham, meaning to bring the three boys to the Priory for the week-end, but the headmaster would only allow them out for Easter Monday. Florence arranged to send for them early on Monday morning and they drove back to Balham. Charles Bravo had had a tennis court laid out and was superintending the putting up of the net. He had a vigorous game with the butler, and when the boys arrived on Monday morning he at once started to play with them. He wrote a letter to his father (those daily letters which telephone conversations now replace) saying that he had "loafed vigorously" and thoroughly enjoyed the week-end.

To help Florence's recovery, they had decided to go to Worthing, and to take a house there as more comfortable than lodgings. On Tuesday, April 18, Mrs. Cox set off to Worthing to find a suitable house. Good living was the rule of the Priory and Mrs. Cox took a flask of sherry with her to recruit her in her exertions. Meanwhile Florence ordered the carriage to drive in to town and her husband was to accompany her. The carriage turned out of the gates into Bedford Hill Road and when a few minutes later it passed Orwell Lodge Florence turned her head away in the gesture that had become instinctive. Charles Bravo noticed it and said savagely: "Do you see anybody?" "No," she said. He then muttered some abuse of Dr. Gully, and she exclaimed that he was very unkind to be always bringing up that name after the solemn promise he had made never to refer to the past. He would not like it, she said, if she were to be always taunting him about that woman! Her husband was touched by this, and asked her to forgive him. Then he said pleadingly: "Kiss me!" She was too much ruffled, and refused; whereupon, she afterwards declared, he exclaimed: "Then you shall see what I will do when we get home!" This frightened her, she said, and she did kiss him.

The carriage put him down at the Turkish Baths in Jermyn Street, and then took her to the Haymarket Stores, where she did some shopping. She drove back to the Priory for lunch. Charles Bravo lunched with a friend at St. James's Hall, and came back to Balham in the afternoon. Florence gave him some tobacco she had bought him at the Stores, and he was very much pleased by the little gift, which was indeed a gesture of reconciliation, since in the 'seventies the mistress of the house, so far from encouraging smoking, was understood barely to tolerate it. Charles Bravo said he would now go and smoke in his room, for it was out of the question that he should do it in his wife's drawing-room or morning-room. Florence thought that he would spend the time up there till dinner, but, to her surprise, in the late afternoon he came down dressed for riding and said he was going out on Cremorne. His horsemanship was characteristic of him; he rode badly but with pertinacity and courage. This was the first evening that Florence had stayed up to dinner since her illness, but the meal, which should have been a little domestic celebration, did not go off well. First, Charles Bravo arrived home much shaken, saying the cob had run away with him. The groom told him it was his own fault for riding it on a snaffle instead of a curb. Charles admitted this and said he would not do so next time. When

The Balham Mystery

he came in he looked pale and complained of stiffness. Florence said he must have a mustard bath and sent the butler upstairs to get it ready. She then went upstairs herself to dress. Meanwhile the butler, having prepared his master's bath, came down to the dining-room to finish laying the table. A bottle of burgundy was decanted and placed in the middle of the table. Dinner had to be kept back because Mrs. Cox had not returned, but she arrived a little after half-past seven. She went upstairs, but did not stay to dress as it was too late. When she came down a few minutes afterwards they all went into the dining-room.

The meal was a simple one: whiting, roast lamb and a dish of eggs and anchovies. Charles Bravo seemed unwell and was certainly ill-humoured. Mrs. Cox produced a photograph of the house she had chosen, but he brushed it aside, and said the whole project of going there was an unnecessary expense. Then he was annoyed because a letter from a stockbroker addressed to himself had been sent by mistake to his stepfather. The letter gave an account of some very mild flutters in which Charles had engaged and showed that he had lost twenty pounds. The elder Mr. Bravo disapproved of gambling on the Stock Exchange even to such a trivial extent as this, and he forwarded the letter with a few grave observations of his own. Charles Bravo was the more irritated because his stepfather had had no business to see the letter, anyway. He said he should "write the governor a shirty letter about it". The butler noticed that his master was pale and quite unlike himself, and put it down to the shock of being bolted with; but though he did not complain of it that evening, Charles had been suffering a good deal from toothache and this trouble may have accounted for some of his pallor and moroseness. He drank three glasses of burgundy, about his usual measure. The ladies, it is somewhat startling to learn, drank nearly two bottles of sherry between them.

Six Criminal Women

At a little after half-past eight Charles told his wife she had sat up long enough for a first evening. She agreed and went upstairs, followed by Mrs. Cox, but half-way up the staircase she asked Mrs. Cox to bring her up another glass of sherry. Mrs. Cox at once returned for it to the dining-room and carried it upstairs. She helped Florence to undress, because Mary Ann Keeber, who would ordinarily have done so, was now at her supper. It therefore happened that the two women were quite alone on the first floor, from just after half-past eight until Charles Bravo came upstairs at about half-past nine.

Mary Ann was going upstairs to Mrs. Bravo's bedroom at the same time, and she stood back to let her master go up first. She particularly noted his distraught appearance. He was extremely pleasant and friendly with servants, and it was unlike him to walk upstairs with one of them without speaking. As it was, he looked round at her twice, and she thought he seemed angry. It must be admitted, however, that this would describe the appearance of a man gnawed by toothache. He went to his bedroom and she went to Mrs. Bravo's. Florence asked the girl to bring her a glass of Marsala from the dining-room. Mary Ann went downstairs and returned with half a tumbler full. The master followed her into the bedroom and began to reproach his wife with taking too much wine. As she always took a glass of sherry while she was dressing, she had now swallowed more than a bottleful and half a tumbler of Marsala in the course of the evening. Mary Ann had discreetly gone away into the dressing-room, where she was busy in tidying away Florence's clothes. When she had finished, she went back to Florence's bedroom. Florence was lying in bed, and Mrs. Cox was sitting at the bedside. Mary Ann was accustomed to seeing her sitting there. The maid asked if anything more were wanted and Mrs. Cox said softly, "No", and asked her to take the dogs downstairs. Mary Ann collected the two small

The Balham Mystery

dogs who were in the bedroom and was half-way down the stairs with them when Charles Bravo appeared at the door of his room in desperate plight, calling loudly: "Florence! Florence! Hot water!"

The startled maid turned back and ran to the big bedroom. Strange as it might appear, Mrs. Cox had not heard these frantic cries which were uttered a few feet away from her. She still sat dreamily in her post by the bed. In the bed, Florence, overcome by the fumes of alcohol, was already fast asleep.

Roused by Mary Ann, Mrs. Cox bustled off to Charles Bravo's room, and as she and the maid came in they saw him standing at the window, vomiting. Mrs. Cox at once sent Mary Ann down to the kitchen for a can of hot water. When the girl came back with it Bravo was lying on the floor and Mrs. Cox was rubbing his chest. She now told Mary Ann to go for mustard, for an emetic, and in the course of her errand Mary Ann, thinking it strange the wife should not have been called to a husband in such an alarming crisis, went into Mrs. Bravo's bedroom and succeeded in rousing her from her stupor. As soon as Florence could be made to understand what had happened, she hurried on her dressing-gown and rushed to the spare room. From that moment everyone who saw her agreed that her behaviour was that of a completely innocent woman, distracted with anxiety at her husband's state. Mrs. Cox had sent one of the servants for Dr. Harrison of Streatham, but Mrs. Bravo now insisted on Dr. Moore's being sent for, since he was much the nearer, as he lived in Balham itself.

When Dr. Harrison arrived, Mrs. Cox met him in the hall and told him she was sure Charlie had taken chloroform. She said afterwards that she had not mentioned this to Dr. Moore because the latter was a local man and Charlie would not wish anyone in the neighbourhood to know what he had done. Harrison at once went up to join his colleague and they both tried to detect any odour of chloroform on the patient's breath, but there was none.

In her recent illness Florence had been attended by Mr. Royes Bell of Harley Street, who was a connection of her husband's and an intimate friend of the Bravo family. She now suggested that he should be sent for. Dr. Harrison wrote a note asking Mr. Royes Bell to come at once and to bring someone with him. This note was given to the coachman, who drove with it to Harley Street, and at the end of the two hours necessary to go and come, returned bringing Mr. Royes Bell and Dr. Johnson.

Meantime Florence, with every sign of passionate distress, threw herself on the bed beside her husband; but, weak from illness, overpowered by grief and having had far too much to drink, she soon fell asleep. Dr. Harrison roused her and got her off the bed; he was afraid she would interfere with the sick man's breathing. Presently Charles Bravo came to again; he began to vomit, and the doctors could now be sure that he had taken a strong dose of irritant poison. When Mr. Royes Bell and Dr. Johnson were brought up to the bedroom and had made their examination, Mr. Royes Bell took advantage of the patient's returning consciousness to ask him what he had taken. "I took some laudanum for toothache," he said. "Laudanum will not account for your symptoms," said Dr. Johnson.

Mrs. Cox now glided up to Mr. Royes Bell and, drawing him aside, she made the extraordinary statement that when she had answered Charles Bravo's cries for help he had said: "I have taken poison. Don't tell Florence." Royes Bell was astonished that she had not said so at once. "It's no good sending for a doctor if you don't tell him what's the matter," he said, and hurriedly returned to his colleagues with the news. Dr. Harrison was extremely annoyed that Mrs. Cox had not made the disclosure to him. Mrs. Cox, blandly obstinate, replied that she had done so. "I told you when

The Balham Mystery

you arrived," she said. "You did nothing of the sort," replied Dr. Harrison heatedly; "you said he had taken chloroform." The night passed with no improvement and at five o'clock in the morning Dr. Harrison, Dr. Moore and Dr. Johnson went home, the latter taking with him a specimen of the vomit for analysis. Mr. Royes Bell, who was now in charge of the case, remained at the Priory.

The day was Wednesday, April 19. It wore on slowly, the patient suffering agonies of pain succeeded by periods of profound exhaustion. During one of his calmer moments he saw his wife bending over him. A memory seemed to cross him of their miserable altercation in the carriage. "Kiss me!" he pleaded. She did so. Many times during the day he asked her to kiss him. At noon he had a short will made in which he left her everything, and he told Royes Bell that if his mother arrived too late to see him alive she must be given a message from him. It was: "Be kind to Florence."

At three o'clock that afternoon the three doctors, once more gathered at his bed, tried again to make him say whether he had taken anything. The butler heard his master exclaim in weak but irritable accents: "Why the devil should I have sent for you if I knew what was the matter with me?"

That same afternoon old Mr. and Mrs. Bravo, who had been telegraphed for, arrived from St. Leonards. They brought with them Mr. Bravo's brother-in-law, Dr. Henry Smith, Miss Bell, the surgeon's sister, and their maid Amelia Bushell, who had known Charles from a small child. Mrs. Cox met them at the station with the appalling news that Charles had poisoned himself. The whole party disbelieved it, and Mr. Bravo stoutly denied that such a thing was possible.

When they arrived at the Priory, Mrs. Bravo told Florence that she had always nursed Charles in all his ailments and begged that she might take charge of the sickroom now.

Six Criminal Women

Florence, distracted and incapable, agreed willingly. She gave up the double bedroom to the Bravos and went upstairs to share Mrs. Cox's.

Next morning, Thursday, the twentieth, there was no alteration and very little hope, and Florence, acting on a natural impulse, sent Mrs. Cox round to Orwell Lodge. She afterwards said pathetically that she had always thought Dr. Gully "the cleverest doctor in the world". When everyone else had failed, she instinctively turned for help to him. There was no room for embarrassment. Mrs. Cox presented herself boldly, and Pritchard, putting her in the drawing-room, went to announce her to his master. "You shouldn't have let her in, Pritchard," said Dr. Gully, but he went to see what was the matter. When he heard the trouble, he suggested mustard plaster, and small doses of arsenicum. Within five minutes of her arrival Mrs. Cox was walking down the drive again.

Meanwhile Florence, in her desperate search for succour, had bethought her of a friend of her father's, the famous Sir William Gull. This doctor, who was short-tempered and domineering, and bore a curious resemblance to Napoleon, was the most eminent physician of the day and was considered to be unrivalled in diagnosis. Though, as Mr. Royes Bell was in charge of the case, she ought not to have summoned another doctor without consulting him, the distraught wife sent Sir William Gull a note saying her husband was desperately ill and could he come at once? This note made no mention of poison.

Sir William Gull and Mr. Royes Bell agreed to ignore this breach of etiquette and they drove out to Balham together, arriving at the Priory at six o'clock that evening. When Sir William Gull entered the bedroom he told everybody to leave it except the five other doctors there already. Then he made his examination. Bending over Charles Bravo, he said: "This is not disease. You have been poisoned. Pray tell us

The Balham Mystery

how you came by it." In weak but unfaltering tones the dying man swore solemnly that he had taken nothing except laudanum for his toothache. "You have taken a great deal more than that," said Sir William Gull. Dr. Johnson from his post at the foot of the bed said that if the patient could tell them no more, someone might be accused of poisoning him. "I cannot help that," said Charles Bravo; "I have taken nothing else."

Mrs. Cox had already made two statements, to Dr. Harrison and Mr. Royes Bell, each one more important than the last. She now capped them with a third to Sir William Gull. She explained that what Charles Bravo had really said to her was: "I have taken poison for Gully. Don't tell Florence." How Sir William Gull received this is not known, but he, alone of the seven doctors, inclined to the theory of suicide. Dr. Johnson's analysis of the vomit proved useless, for it had been tested for arsenic only, of which it contained no trace. It appeared at first as if no other specimen were obtainable, for when Mary Ann had attended Charles Bravo in his first seizure Mrs. Cox had ordered her to wash the basin and throw away the contents. However, Sir William Gull stood at the window from which he had been told that Charles Bravo had vomited, and he saw traces of the rejected matter on the leads beneath. He ordered some to be collected and took it back with him to London. He had left the sickroom for a few moments only when he was hastily called back; but the patient only wanted to repeat his solemn assurance that he had not poisoned himself and to ask if there were any hope? Sir William Gull would not deceive him. He told him that he was half dead already. To the parents he said he doubted if their son would last the night. He then left the Priory and his prognostication was soon fulfilled.

At four o'clock on the morning of April 21 Charles Bravo died, within five months of his wedding day.

Six Criminal Women

In the shock of grief, terror and dismay that swept the household, the only person to remain calm, useful, practical and thoughtful for others was Mrs. Cox. There could be no question of granting a death certificate, and it was realized that a coroner's inquest must be prepared for. The coroner for East Surrey was Mr. Carter, and Mrs. Cox at once got into touch with him. She gave him to understand that this was a case of suicide and that it was an object to spare the family's feelings as far as possible. She suggested that the inquest should be held in the Priory itself, to avoid distressing publicity, and added, with her usual attention to detail, that refreshments would be provided for the jurors. Mr. Carter fell in with these arrangements in the most obliging way. No notice of the inquest was sent to any of the papers, and no reporters were present. The ceremony, conducted in the pleasant seclusion of the Priory dining-room, was almost a family affair, except that a few of the late Charles Bravo's barrister friends had wormed themselves in. However, no one paid them any attention.

The proceedings opened on April 28, and the coroner had clearly taken it for granted that the case was one of suicide about which it would be well to say as little as might be. Meanwhile, however, the pathologist to whom Sir William Gull had submitted the specimen for analysis had revealed the fact that Charles Bravo had died from a large dose of antimony, taken in the form of tartar emetic. On the advice of Dr. Smith, Mr. Bravo took this report to Scotland Yard, who sent down Inspector Clarke to see if he could trace tartar emetic in the possession of anyone in the Priory. This he entirely failed to do. The rooms both of Mrs. Bravo and Mrs. Cox were full of patent medicines, but all of a quite harmless character. Meanwhile, evidence was given at the inquest that was difficult to reconcile with the idea of suicide, for Mary Ann Keeber showed that the couple were on terms of devoted affection, and Mr. Royes Bell repeated the im-

The Balham Mystery

pressive denials of the victim that he had taken anything to poison himself. Nevertheless, Mr. Carter appeared anxious to hurry through a verdict in accordance with his own view. He refused to hear the testimony of Dr. Moore and Dr. Johnson, both of whom wanted to speak, and he refused to allow Florence to be called, as he understood that she was prostrated by shock. The jury, however, were far from satisfied. They returned a verdict to the effect that Charles Bravo had died from a dose of tartar emetic but that there was no proof as to how he had come by it.

The next day, April 29, the funeral took place at Norwood cemetery, and on the thirtieth, Florence retired with Mrs. Cox to Brighton, where Mrs. Cox had found them apartments at 38 Brunswick Terrace. Mr. Joseph Bravo remained at the Priory, and he had all his son's drawers sealed up. Florence heard of this in her retreat, and she at once wrote to her father-in-law about it. She said that all her husband's possessions belonged now to her, and no one else had the right to touch "one single thing". At the same time she took the opportunity of suggesting to Mr. Bravo that any money he had been in the habit of giving his son should now be considered as due to her. "What he died possessed of I must leave to you; he told me that he had two hundred pounds a year from investments, and of course his books and pictures and private papers at Palace Green are now mine. . . . P.S. Poor Charlie told me that you promised to allow him eight hundred pounds a year."

Such a letter, at such a time, does not put her in an amiable light; but a childish greed and selfishness was the reverse side of her emotional nature. Charles Bravo had insisted, with brutal and insulting harshness, that all her possessions should be his; he had said if he were not to have everything for his own then he would not marry her at all. She had acquiesced at the time, but now she was particularly alive to the idea that she ought to reap her side of the bargain.

Six Criminal Women

She wrote a little later apologizing to Mr. Bravo for the disagreeable tone of her last letter; she had quite misunderstood his intentions, she said; she added that a letter from Mr. Royes Bell had convinced her that poor Charlie had committed suicide, and she believed it had been because "that dreadful woman" had been pressing him for money; this, too, was why he had been so anxious to cut down their expenses. This was the letter of a woman who was either genuinely stupid or a very incompetent deceiver. There had been no trouble from Charles Bravo's mistress, who had made no claim on him at all; she would not have got very far with such a man if she had; whereas the cutting down of expenses required no explanation beyond the fact that Charles Bravo was exceedingly careful about money and was supported by a woman who disliked and disapproved of her daughter-in-law.

Dissatisfaction with the conduct of the inquest was growing. It showed itself in a flood of anonymous letters which reached Florence in her rooms at Brunswick Terrace, but it was also making its way among the reputable part of society. One of Charles Bravo's friends who had been present at the inquest, a Mr. Willoughby, went and explained his uneasiness at Scotland Yard; while several newspapers, notably the *Telegraph,* began an agitation to have the proceedings reopened. Florence felt herself to be in a position of odious notoriety, which threatened to become something worse. On her father's advice she published the offer of a rewards of five hundred pounds to anyone who could prove the sale of tartar emetic in the neighbourhood of the Priory.

The result of the pressure that was brought to bear was that an enquiry was held at the Treasury, at which Mrs. Bravo and Mrs. Cox each made a voluntary statement. The latter's was so startling that a second inquest was ordered to take place on July 11.

This time it was entirely out of private hands. Far from

The Balham Mystery

the pleasant seclusion of the Priory dining-room, the jurors met in the billiard-room of the Bedford Hotel, outside Balham Station. It was very hot, and the billiard-room windows were open, with the Venetian blinds half down. Public interest was enormous. Every available inch of space not occupied by the performers of the inquest was filled with a mob of intensely curious spectators. The possible issues were of the utmost seriousness, and the persons chiefly concerned were all able to pay for the best legal assistance, and consequently a most impressive collection of counsel was assembled in these incongruous surroundings. The Crown counsel were Sir John Holker, Mr. Gorst, Q.C., and Mr., afterwards Sir, Harry Poland. For Mrs. Charles Bravo there appeared Sir Henry James, Q.C., and Mr. Biron; and Florence had also retained Mr. Murphy, Q.C., to act for Mrs. Cox. Mr. Joseph Bravo was represented by Mr. Lewis, a partner of Messrs. Lewis & Lewis, the famous firm of solicitors. Half-way through, the proceedings took such an ominous turn that Mr. Sergeant Parry and Mr. Archibald Smith presented themselves, saying they had been instructed to watch the case for Dr. Gully.

The legal gentlemen were indeed eminent, so eminent that they defied all control. In a court of law a judge would have managed them, but in the billiard-room of the Bedford Hotel there was nobody but Mr. Carter. His unhappy position was rather that of Phaeton, who attempted to drive the coursers of the sun and was tumbled ignominiously into the ocean.

Before the inquest opened a macabre ceremony was performed. It was necessary for the jurors to view the body, and the coffin was therefore taken up out of its brick vault in Norwood cemetery and placed on wooden blocks under a canvas shelter. That the formality of viewing might be accomplished, the undertakers had cut away a square of the lead casing and left the dead man's face in sight under a pane of glass. The face was as dark as a mummy's, the teeth, exposed by rigor, were entirely black. The jurors filed past the coffin, raising their tall hats as they did so. A heavy, overpowering smell of disinfectants added to the oppressiveness of the sultry day.

The inquest was considered afterwards to have been conducted in a most undisciplined manner. Not only was Mr. Carter unable to control the loud-voiced comments of the crowd or to prevent the jury from making unsuitable demonstrations; he could not prevent the lawyers from extorting by relentless cross-examination, much material that would probably have been ruled as inadmissible in a proper court. A domestic picture of the most graphic detail was built up by the statements of a wide variety of witnesses, but the three most important were Mrs. Bravo, Dr. Gully and Mrs. Cox.

In Mrs. Cox's examination, which was the longest, she quietly and persistently maintained that Charles Bravo had committed suicide and that he had done so out of retrospective jealousy of Dr. Gully. Her story which had grown in circumstantial detail from the time she made her first communication to Dr. Harrison now received its crowning touch. She said that at one of the moments when she was alone with Charles he had said: "Why did you tell them?" and she had answered: "I had to tell them. I could not let you die." The only creature who could have contradicted her was now a blackened corpse. When she was asked why she had not at once reported that Charles Bravo had said he had taken poison "for Dr. Gully", she replied that it had been with a view of shielding Mrs. Bravo's character.

As she and Florence both adhered to this story of the death, the story of the liaison with Dr. Gully was pushed forward into a position of the utmost importance. It acquired in fact an importance in the minds of the lawyers which Mrs. Cox had perhaps not foreseen, for if the liaison could

The Balham Mystery

account for the suicide, if still existing, it might equally be held to account for a murder. This perhaps accounts for the remarkable lengths to which the Crown counsel and Mr. Lewis went in attempting to find out when the relationship had begun—a matter, after all, of some four years before Charles Bravo and Florence had ever set eyes on each other. When Mrs. Cox was asked twice over whether she was not aware of the fact that her employer and Dr. Gully were lovers, she looked down and gently brushed the tablecloth with her gloved hand. She admitted at last that she had suspected it. She was now called upon sharply to speak up, and this request was received with clamorous delight by the onlookers. Mr. Sergeant Parry was appalled by these proceedings. "Applause in a court of justice!" he exclaimed. "It is terrible! It is fearful!" But Mr. Carter was helpless.

When Florence Bravo was called her appearance created a sensation. In her widow's dress of black crêpe, her bright hair strained back under a bonnet with a crêpe veil, her large blue eyes sunken in her pale face, she appeared on the verge of breaking down, but she spoke with unexpected firmness, until Mr. Lewis, after a long cross-examination on her relations with Dr. Gully, began with savage persistence to demand at what point they had begun. She denied that this had been while she was at Malvern, but Mr. Lewis produced a letter she had written six years ago to a maid called Laundon, in which she promised to recommend her to another place and said, "I hope you will never mention what passed at Malvern." "What did that mean, Mrs. Bravo?" asked Mr. Lewis and he repeated the question until his merciless reiteration broke her self-control. Sobbing wildly, she implored the coroner for protection, which he was powerless to extend. He could not control the counsel any more than she could.

Dr. Gully's examination aroused a great deal of unfavourable comment, both in the press and at the actual scene of the inquest, where several jurors showed disapproval because the coroner allowed him to sit down during his lengthy ordeal. There was by the end of the proceedings no shred of evidence, no shade of implication, to connect him with the crime, but public opinion was weighted against him almost as if he had been proved a murderer. It was of course right that so serious a breach of professional etiquette, particularly on the part of such an eminent man, should be strongly condemned, but the tragedy of Dr. Gully's fall after a long and distinguished career seems to have passed unregarded. This was no doubt partly or even largely due to the fact that a fellow human being always arouses hostility and resentment if he or she is felt to have enjoyed a sexual success out of proportion to any physical or social advantages. That Dr. Gully, a man well over sixty, should have had a pretty young woman as his adoring mistress, unloosed a flood of vindictive taunts and scathing vituperation.

Once the discreditable fact had been admitted in its full culpability the rest of Dr. Gully's evidence was that of an upright, distinguished man with every instinct of a gentleman. He spoke honestly, simply, and with a keen sense of regret for his backsliding. "Too true, sir, too true," he said, when the Crown counsel flung his past indiscretion in his face. At one point of the proceedings the horrible implication was made that he had prescribed medicines for Mrs. Ricardo to bring on a miscarriage. His prescriptions had been traced to the chemists who dispensed them. Dr. Gully replied with effective simplicity that to any medical man the prescriptions would speak for themselves; they were not such as would be used to procure abortion. All his evidence went to show, just as Florence Bravo's had shown, that after she had dismissed him in October of 1875 he had never attempted to have any further communication with her. He had seen her once at her own request, when he advised her to give way about the marriage settlement. After that, he had

The Balham Mystery

never even laid eyes on her. Nor, apart from the one interview in the coachman's lodge, had she ever attempted to get into touch with him till she sent Mrs. Cox to ask his advice for her dying husband. He had prescribed for her pains, and he had sent her a bottle of laurel water: both these acts had been brought about by the agency of Mrs. Cox.

The dead man, according to the pathologist, had taken the enormous quantity of some forty grains of antimony, and a thorough search of the Priory, including the medicine chests of Mrs. Bravo and Mrs. Cox and the numerous bottles that were littered about in both ladies' rooms, had revealed no trace of anything likely to contain antimony in any form. The reward of five hundred pounds offered by Florence to anyone who could prove a sale of tartar emetic in the neighbourhood had produced no response. But now it came to light that a large amount of tartar emetic had been on the premises no later than the preceding January, three months before Charles Bravo's death. The then coachman at the Priory, Griffiths, had bought tartar emetic to doctor Florence's horses, and he had also used it in Dr. Gully's stables at Malvern. Dr. Gully had not known of this; he had forbidden Griffiths to physic the horses, as he himself treated them by hydropathy, "with marvellous results". In the Priory stables, however, Griffiths had it all his own way, and he made a profuse purchase of tartar emetic, regardless of the fact that he had only four horses under his charge. He was asked why he had bought physic enough for at least a hundred, and he explained that he liked to have things by him. On the day of the Lord Mayor's Show, 1875, he was driving his mistress, accompanied of course by Mrs. Cox, in the London streets, and the carriage was involved in a serious collision. Griffiths denied that he was to blame, but Charles Bravo, harsh, impetuous and alarmed for Florence's safety, insisted on his being dismissed. He left the Priory in January. Griffiths bore Charles Bravo a bitter grudge in consequence, though he went at once into the service of Lady Prescott. He said that while the tartar emetic was in his possession he had kept it locked in a cupboard in the harness room, and that before he left he had poured it down a drain in the stable yard. Unfortunately, though there was no reason to suppose Griffiths a deliberate liar, he was excitable and loquacious and his evidence was full of contradictions and inconsistencies. That he said he had kept the poison locked up and thrown away the remainder before he left was nothing like so significant as the fact that a large quantity of tartar emetic had actually been on the premises.

It was an accepted fact that Charles Bravo must have taken the poison in some form of drink after the dinner hour of seven-thirty. As Florence had gone upstairs immediately after dinner, no coffee had been served that evening. Therefore the two mediums in which he could have taken the poison were the Burgundy he drank at dinner or the water in the bottle on his bedroom washstand from which he always drank a glassful before going to bed. The medical evidence inclined to its having been taken in the water, and this view was supported by the fact that the butler had been near at hand, in dining-room or hall, ever since the wine was decanted some half an hour before dinner. Though it would not have been impossible, it would have been exceedingly difficult for anyone to enter the dining-room and doctor the Burgundy unobserved. But with regard to the water in the bedroom: Florence and Mrs. Cox had the first floor entirely to themselves between the time of their going upstairs at eight-thirty and Charles Bravo and Mary Ann's appearance at about half-past nine. The matter could have been decided by the examination of what remained of wine and water; but by the same perverse good fortune which had supported the criminal in every aspect of the crime the remains of wine and water could, neither of them, be accounted for. The butler had opened a fresh bottle of Burgundy for Dr. Harri-

The Balham Mystery

son and Dr. Moore; he could not say what had happened to the remains of the other; the house had been in confusion and he could not remember if anyone had drunk it or not. (Similarly he would not, of course, have known if anyone had poured it away.) The remains of the water bottle had not been noticed either. The doctors had noticed the bottle in the room, but at that time they had naturally attached no importance to it. They were not continuously present with the patient, and any careful, attentive soul refilling the bottle with fresh water would scarcely attract attention.

The verdict which was finally pronounced after the sittings had lasted three weeks was that Charles Bravo had not died by misadventure and not committed suicide, but that he had been poisoned, though there was not sufficient evidence to say by whom. This statement came as a stunning blow, because it at once branded Mrs. Cox as a liar, and therefore it was next door to an indictment of murder of either herself or Florence or both, with the possibility of suspicion resting upon Dr. Gully. The pamphlet, *The Balham Mystery,* is exceptionally interesting, as it not only supplies an exhaustive account of the proceedings at the inquest and drawings of the scenes and people involved, but it conveys the public feeling of the time in three fanciful drawings, crude and morbid and of astonishing effectiveness. One is of the devil dressed as a showman at a fair, with three thimbles standing on a board. The drawing is headed: "Rather a Poser. Under which thimble is the P——?" Does P stand for poisoner? At all events there is no doubt as to whom the three thimbles represent. The second of these full-page drawings is in vivid chiaroscuro. It shows the setting sun from which a stony road leads up to the foreground. Here in deep shadow a gallows stands, and beneath it, sitting at the edge of an open pit strewn with bones, is a figure of such terror as is seldom seen outside nightmare. The hooded cloak reveals one hoof, and a head that would be a skull except that the features are still there. The expression of intense personal misery such as the devil might be supposed to bear is combined with an indrawn, waiting look and a hideous smile. On the lap a skeleton hand holds a whip. The picture is called: "Waiting for the culprit." But even more interesting is a small illustration at the end. This is a murky-looking corner where several phials and a glass jar containing what looks like an anatomical specimen are standing on a shelf. A single beam of light illuminates a woman's hand which stretches out towards one of the small bottles. A careful examination of the drawings of Mrs. Bravo and Mrs. Cox shows that the sleeve, banded with dark ribbon and finished with a deep fall of lace, is not identifiable with any dress which either of them is shown as wearing; but it is an elegant hand, with a massive bracelet on the wrist; this, and the richness of the sleeve, suggests inescapably that it is meant for Florence Bravo, while the anatomical specimen carries an equally inescapable suggestion of Dr. Gully.

There are two authoritative pronouncements on this crime which after seventy years still holds its secret. In his memoir of Sir Harry Poland, *Seventy-two Years at the Bar,* Mr. Ernest Rowlands says that Sir Harry Poland told him that he had his theory, though it was not for publication, and there was not enough evidence for a prosecution. It is tantalizing to read such words, because this theory, formed by a man who was one of the counsel, would be as near to the actual truth as the rest of us could hope ever to come. But Sir Harry Poland's other observations are extremely interesting. He entirely exonerates Dr. Gully, and he mentions a possible motive for each of the women: that Mrs. Cox was threatened by Charles Bravo with the loss of her pleasant life at the Priory to which the alternative was drudgery and insecurity and the anxiety for her sons' future, and that Mrs. Bravo murdered her husband to avoid losing her

The Balham Mystery

companion, but he says that the first motive was scarcely sufficient and the second was not credible. Nevertheless the effect of that paragraph is that he thought it was the motive rather than identity of the culprit which remained obscure.

Sir John Hall in *The Bravo Mystery and other Cases* also clears Dr. Gully from all suspicion of complicity in the murder and says that there is no evidence of Florence Bravo's having wanted to renew her liaison, of her having procured poison, or behaved in any way but one natural to an affectionate and single-hearted wife; but he also says that what lays her open to grave suspicion is the way in which she supported every statement of Mrs. Cox, and the extraordinary intimacy in which she lived with her; not only were they the closest friends, but for the last fortnight they had been sleeping in the same bed. Sir John Hall says: "If one be guilty the other cannot be innocent."

It would be presumptuous to hazard any theory which was not closely conformable with what has been said by these two writers, but it is, one hopes, not going beyond the lines thus laid down to say that the murder was certainly done and almost certainly planned by Mrs. Cox, and that all that is doubtful is her motive for it. The Marxist trend of present-day thought perhaps inclines our generation to attach more importance to economic motive than the men of Sir Harry Poland's day were prepared to allow. To us it does not seem incredible that a woman of such calibre as Mrs. Cox should be prepared to commit murder in order to maintain her own security and that of her children. On the other hand, it seems likely that though Florence Bravo did not know that the crime was to be committed at that time, or, perhaps, that it was ever actually to be committed at all she knew afterwards how and by whom it had been done. Though very little is known of her subsequent story, that little is of extreme significance: it is simply that she died within fourteen months of the second inquest. It is not generally known whether her support of Mrs. Cox continued during the short remainder of her own life. A theory (in default of any evidence) is sometimes suggested, more or less facetiously, that her death may have been a second murder, but by far the most probable explanation is that after the second inquest the truth about her husband's death became known to her, and that the strain of enduring this knowledge was more than she could bear. What is dreadfully clear is the influence of the controlled, secretive, ruthless character over the sensuous, impulsive, helpless one. Had Florence Bravo been another sort of woman she might be thought the victim of some morbid attachment to Mrs. Cox, but the history of her love affair and her marriage puts this out of court. Mrs. Cox dominated her because she ran her house, attended to her wants, promoted her comforts and pleasures and enabled her to lead her life as she wanted to lead it. Mrs. Cox was the evil spirit whose power over us is the power we ourselves have given it. Florence's character, self-indulgent, greedy, impetuous, pleasure-loving, had its exact complement in the character that was vigilant, cautious, hard-working, self-reliant, capable of any self-denial to achieve a particular end, just as her appearance with its Rubens-like colouring, its feminine softness and grace, was the opposite of the plain, dark, unobtrusive figure, which had developed a self-protective obscurity.[1]

In the infinite complexities of the mind it is possible to know without realizing the knowledge, until circumstances force the mind to admit it. In their extreme intimacy before the death of Charles Bravo, when Mrs. Cox nursed her,

[1] A study of Florence Bravo's will in Somerset House bears out the theory that there was a complete rupture between her and Mrs. Cox at some time after the second inquest. The will was drawn in February 1877. It made large and detailed bequests of property and money to various people, including Florence Bravo's goddaughter, the grandchild of Dr. Gully; but Mrs. Cox received nothing whatever and is mentioned in the will only as the mother of the three boys, who were left one hundred pounds each.

waited on her and slept in her bed, Florence must have confided to her friend whatever causes of resentment and dislike she may have had against her husband, and she must have felt assured that her own feelings were met by a profound agreement. Yet nothing would be more natural than that she should accept, at first, Mrs. Cox's version of the tragedy which had overtaken the household when she herself was weak from illness and bemused by a drunken sleep, and that at the actual moment of calamity all her other feelings should be submerged in dismay and terror at the sight of her husband's agonies.

It is of course impossible to say what may have been the extent of her complicity, whether she were an accessory before or after the event, whether her silence were willing or unwilling, but her early death seems to speak volumes on her sufferings. Hers was an organism that collapses in physical ill health whenever it is placed under a nervous strain, and if she ceased to want to live there would be no recovery. The force that killed her husband killed her also.

Mrs. Cox was heard of many years after, visiting an elderly invalid with fruit and flowers. "She was quiet and so *very* kind," said those who remembered her visits.

Dr. Gully died seven years later, and for those remaining years his penance was heavy. During a long life he had built up for himself a position of public respect and admiration such as very few men enjoy. As a result of the disclosures at the Balham inquest this was blasted overnight. Not only was his name trampled on by the public, but he had to bear the ruin of his professional reputation. His name was removed from all the societies to which he belonged and from all the journals and papers to which he had been one of the most distinguished contributors. That he bitterly regretted the love affair that had proved fatal to him, he had said himself; but however much his feelings might have altered towards her, the anguish and death of the woman he had loved must have caused him deep grief. He was a man of unusual gifts of personality and intellect, but, with all his good qualities, he had neglected the Wisdom of Solomon:

"Discretion shall preserve thee, understanding shall keep thee.
"To deliver thee from the strange woman, even from the stranger which flattereth with her tongue.
"Which forsaketh the guide of her youth and forgetteth the covenant of her God.
"For her house inclineth unto death, and her paths unto the dead."